# FLIES THAT CATCH TROUT

# FLIES THAT CATCH TROUT

## TERRY LAWTON

ROBERT HALE · LONDON

© *Terry Lawton 2009*
*First published in Great Britain 2009*

ISBN 978 0 7090 8193 7

Robert Hale Limited
Clerkenwell House
Clerkenwell Green
London EC1R 0HT

www.halebooks.com

*A catalogue record for this book is available from the British Library*

10 9 8 7 6 5 4 3 2 1

Design by Judy Linard
Printed in China and arranged by New Era Printing Co Ltd, Hong Kong

# CONTENTS

# ACKNOWLEDGEMENTS

MANY READERS may imagine that researching a book like this, with much of the time spent during the author's closed season without the distraction of fishing, would be relatively easy. But the winter in the northern hemisphere is show time in the USA and the middle of the northern winter is the height of the season in the southern hemisphere. That means that guides and others are out on the river all day and every day, well away from their computers and e-mail – catching trophy fish.

But I got there in the end and could not have done so without an extraordinary amount of help and kindness from fellow fly fishers around the world, many of whom were only names to me; sadly I probably will never get to meet many of them. But I really do appreciate your help and involvement with this book.

One of the many people from around the world who contributed, and who deserves a special mention, is my local fly-tying mentor Richard Slaughter. Richard tied the flies which I was not able to source from the original tiers, some of whom are, sadly, no longer tying or have died. I hope that readers will appreciate his hard working in tying and recreating some historic flies very accurately.

All of the following, some good fishing friends, others recipients of demanding e-mails and letters from me, have contributed to this book: James Andersson, Barry and Cathy Beck, Lennart Bergqvist, Tony Biggs, Russell Blessing, Roger Butler, Mary Carter-Hepworth, Pete Carty, Bill Dod, Ed Engle, Mark Forslund, Marjan Fratnik, Thommy Gustavsson, Mick Hall, Gary Harlen, Peter Hayes, Matti Huitila, Randall Kaufmann, Rick Keam, Johan Klingberg,

Hans van Klinken, Mel Krieger, Andrew Levy, Eduardo Marino, Craig Mathews, Marcelo Morales, Stevie Munn, Ken Orr, Jens Pilgaard, Derek Quilliam, Clark Reid, Alan Shepherd, Alan Simmons, Mats Sjostrand, Rob Sloane, Tom Sutcliffe, Abel Tripoli, Al and Martha Troth, Anssi Uitti, Hans Weilenmann, Peter Whiting, Dave and Emily Whitlock, and Dick Winter.

My thanks for various quotations go to: Mike Stevens of Stevens Publishing for material from *The Fly* by R.H. Wigram; Rob Sloane of FlyLife Publishing for *Australia's Best Trout Flies*; Nick Sawyer for quotations from Frank Sawyer's works; *Country Life* magazine for *Going Fishing* by Negley Farson; Stackpole Books for *Lee Wulff on Flies*; and The Flyfisher's Classic Library for *Grayling and How to Catch Them* and *Recollections of a Sportsman* by Francis M. Walbran.

Every effort has been made to contact copyright holders but apologies are extended to any author who may believe that he should have been consulted.

# ILLUSTRATIONS

# CREDITS

ALL FLY PHOTOGRAPHS are by Chris Hoelzer with the exception of the
photograph of the original Hidy flymph which was taken by Johan Klingberg.
Other photographs were taken by Tom Sutcliffe, Stevie Munn, James Andersson
and the author. My thanks go to one and all.

# FLY TIERS

Russell Blessing
Mark Forslund
Marjan Fratnik
Mick Hall
Matti Huitila
Rick Keam
Johan Klingberg
Hans van Klinken
Mel Krieger
Terry Lawton
Jésus Héctor Léoni
Marcelo Morales

Stevie Munn
Ken Orr
Jens Pilgaard
Derek Quilliam
Adrian Reboratti
Diana Reboratti
Clark Reid
Alan Simmons
Richard Slaughter
Tom Sutcliffe
Hans Weilenmann

# INTRODUCTION

IN HIS BOOK *Lee Wulff on Flies*, the late Lee Wulff wrote: 'Each fly is a dream we cast out to fool fish. These flies in which we have the most faith we fish with more hope, more determination and for longer periods. Because we give these flies the best chance they are the ones that catch most of the fish for us.' Every fly fisherman has personal favourites, flies that inspire confidence, many shared with a multitude of fellow anglers. But some will be less well known because they are old patterns that are nearly forgotten or perhaps came from a far-off land. I hope that the selection of trout flies in this book will meet with approval and that some of the less obvious patterns will find a place in some fly boxes, perhaps belonging to more adventurous anglers.

That old favourite of mine, Jim Jam or Dr J.C. Mottram, wrote some wise words on fly patterns and fly tying in his last book, *Thoughts on Angling*.

*It is remarkable how flies gain a high reputation, are used by a great number of fishermen, then gradually lose favour and, finally, are seldom found in the angler's fly-box. I think the explanation lies in the fact that professional fly-tiers gradually and unconsciously alter the character of the fly until it comes to differ widely from the original and is of no particular interest to the trout.*

He then went on to describe what had happened to the Wickham's Fancy and how it had been bastardized over the years and ended-up with 'its present-day bad reputation'.

Moving forward from 1945, when Mottram's book was published, Hans van Klinken wrote: 'I saw how flies lose their names and change so much that the history and the original dressing just fades away in a only a few years.' He has seen this process happen to his pattern, the Klinkhåmer Special. He admits that he has tried to make every change and choice of materials to try to improve his pattern, but nothing that he did or tried had proved to be better or make the pattern more effective over the years. He still ties the fly with his original choice of materials. I asked Hans why so many Dutch fly fishermen tie such good flies. His answer? 'It's easy to explain. We have terrible weather in late autumn, winter and early spring so many anglers spend a lot of time tying flies.'

Another piece of good advice from Wulff is:

*Tying flies for our sport is like any other complex endeavour. The tier should learn the rules before he breaks them. He should be able to tie the time-tested conventional patterns neatly and well before he brings studied carelessness into his work. Flies have character and fly tiers give it to them.*

During my research for this book, I reached a better understanding of the importance of the sedge, or caddis, in all its forms to fly fishing both at home and around the world, and the growing understanding of the importance of midges to the diet of trout in rivers. I am sure that I am not alone in believing that many anglers would normally associate midges with what are known in England as the buzzers of reservoirs and still waters. But these little insects hatch in their multitudes in rivers and trout, even big ones, eat them in vast quantities. This is part of the reason why more anglers fish tiny flies on the rivers of the Rocky Mountains and elsewhere.

One of the interesting challenges was tracking down the true stories behind the flies in this book and comparing the original tyings to the modern versions. Some patterns had longer histories than I had appreciated, and with others the challenge was to identify the originator. Even with patterns developed over the last twenty or thirty years, it can be difficult to tie things down. Not everyone makes notes of exactly when and where the idea for a new pattern came about. And, of course, some new patterns just come about.

To end with another quote from Lee Wulff: 'Let us love the flies we choose to fish with and hope the fish will love them, too.'

# FOREWORD

EVEN IF THE title of this volume seems slightly laboured, it is about 'Trout-Takers' – flies with proven track records from around the world, and which are often transferable to waters other than those of their origin.

Terry Lawton is a keen and deep researcher – as I know from watching him delve into my own library – and I am delighted to write a few words about this, his third and latest book. He seeks to track down as much direct information as he can, and this was evidenced in his *Nymph Fishing – a History of its Art and Practice* (2005) and *Fly Fishing in Rivers and Streams – Techniques and Tactics* (2007).

Now he tells us about fifty-one fly patterns – Dry 23, Nymph 20 and Wet & Streamers 8 – that we ought to have in our fly boxes. He takes us on a global journey which covers a dozen countries including Argentina, Australia, England, New Zealand, South Africa and the United States, and covering patterns from the Adams to the Zug Bug. Some of these you may know, but there are certainly some you won't – I know I didn't! Whilst there are no step-by-step tying instructions (available in other publications) Terry gives us some tying hints and thoughts on how these flies are to be fished. There are variants of the patterns for as G.E.M. Skues observed, 'the number of ways in which flies can be tied is incredible. There are hardly two books which lay down identical methods unless one is a crib from the other. And of all the methods in which I have experimented, from Walton downwards, I have never come across one which had nothing to recommend it, and I should be glad to be master of them all.'

Anyone bold enough to offer the 'origins' of a fly pattern will from time to time find themselves faced with conflicting accounts – and claimants. Often this arises because a pattern becomes more associated in the public mind with the popularizer rather than its originator. Not all evidence is crystal clear, as when, for example, trying to distinguish across the mists of time between the original innovative creator of a fly or a subsequent varier, developer, publicist or popularizer. To untangle the truth from 'myth' on occasion makes the writer wish for the wisdom of Solomon! All one can do is review the historical evidence available and come down on one side or the other.

Then there are identical or similar creations by tyers miles apart and unbeknownst to each other. For example, Oliver Kite's Imperial, in the form that we know it, is generally accepted as being created by him on Wales' River Teifi in 1962. However, a friend of Kite, fishing the River Doubs in France, subsequently encountered an old peasant angler with a flybox 'crammed full of Imperials', who, when shown a Kite Imperial, simply remarked that he had been making such a fly himself since 1950!

Additionally, there are local flies, rarely seen outside their limited locality, the origins of which are simply lost. The Roman poet Horace, in his Odes, used words that can act as a warning to all our endeavours:

'Vixere fortes ante Agamemnona
Multi: sed omnes illacrimabiles
Urgentur ignotique longa
Nocte, carent quia vate sacro.'

Which translates as 'many heroes lived before Agamemnon, but they are unmourned and unknown, lost in darkness because they lack a dedicated poet.'

Terry is the 'dedicated poet' of the takers and their makers in this book, and he, like Poul Jorgensen can say 'one of my foremost interests is to make sure that history is not forgotten and is passed on to other generations.'

Not all of these patterns are designed to 'hold as t'were the mirror up to nature' (Shakespeare – *Hamlet)*, but as Mick Hall, featured herein, has observed 'the challenge in fly tying is to construct a fly that will do what it is designed to do: a challenge in designing flies that work.'

Will these 'trout-takers' be viewed in years to come as 'timeless ties'? Take them out and try them – you decide! No doubt you will favour some more than others for, as Charles Hallock truthfully noted, 'favourite flies are more apt to be the favourites of the anglers themselves than of the fish they are in quest of.' Yet William Lunn encourages us with the observation that 'the proper fly, properly presented, at the proper time, generally brings forth the proper result'. Then, as with the reply to Lewis B. France's question 'Judge, can you tie a fly?' you may respond 'Not very well; but I will some day, and then I'll make the trout round here think they are eating candy.' True 'Trout-Takers' have that effect.

May your flies be tight and their hackles bright.

ROBERT SPAIGHT

Langworth, Lincolnshire
July 2008

# RED TAG

**The following dressing is the one in Walbran's book.**

HOOK:      Dry fly, size 16–18
THREAD:  Black 6/0
TAG:        Scarlet wool, or dyed swan
BODY:     Two or three green or bronze peacock herls, according to
             hook size
HACKLE:  Bright red cock

# RED TAG

*F.M. Walbran – England*

ACCORDING TO RON BROUGHTON in *The Complete Book of the Grayling*, the Red Tag, which was first tied as a trout fly for low-water conditions in high summer, is the best-known fly for grayling. He suggests that it was then known as the Worcester Gem and was introduced to the trout and grayling rivers and streams of the Yorkshire Dales and used successfully, fished wet, for grayling by F.M. Walbran in 1878. As well as being a top grayling pattern in the UK, with a long history, it is the fly of choice of many a trout fisherman in Australia.

Walbran in his book *Grayling and How to Catch Them* and *Recollections of a Sportsman*, first published in 1895, wrote that grayling showed a preference for flies with 'tags of different hues'. He described them as 'fancy flies' as they bore no resemblance to any form of insect life. He recommended using imitations of naturals up until the sharp frosty nights of November started to clear rivers of natural insects and nymphs. A fly with a red tag could then be fished as the tail, or point, fly. For him the Red Tag was 'the very best among a whole list of fancy grayling flies'. He noted that he sometimes added a turn of gold tinsel under the red tag.

He continued: 'I was the first to introduce it into the Yorkshire rivers, and its marked success soon made it a leading favourite. A Worcester gentleman gave me a pattern among others, in 1878, and the very first time that I used it on the Yore, I killed no less than twenty-five fine grayling through its agency.' Research suggests that the man was a Thomas Flynn, who fished the Teme and invented the Worcester Gem in about 1850. He would probably have fished his fly wet to grayling in the days when dry fly fishing was in its infancy. We can only speculate as to whether or not he tried fishing it dry and to trout. Michael Leighton in his book *Trout Flies of Shropshire and the Welsh Borderlands* suggests that the fly was known as the Worcester Wonder in Worcestershire.

On 10 October 1886, Walbran was fishing the Yore at Tanfield with William Senior, the angling editor of *The Field*, who fished a Red Tag, tied with an ibis tail, dry, and caught four previously uncatchable grayling within half an hour. (H.A. Rolt also included ibis for the tag, or scarlet wool.) This was the first time that Walbran had witnessed grayling being caught on a dry fly. As he fished the Test with F.M. Halford, G.S. Marryat and others, it seems safe to assume that he would have introduced the Red Tag to the river, although on one memorable day with 'H' (as he called Halford) he started by fishing the worm in the mill pool at Houghton Mill.

In his book *Floating Flies and How to Dress Them*, first published in 1886, F.M. Halford included the Red Tag in his list of fly patterns. He described it as 'a grand grayling pattern when fished dry' and referred to 'a new and very killing pattern of the Red Tag, dressed with blood-red hackle, Ibis tag, and body of a single strand of the blue and yellow macaw tail-feather that has been lately introduced by Mr Marryat'.

When *Australia's Best Trout Flies* was published in 1997, one of the most popular dry flies was the Red Tag, including a deer hair variant, which was listed as a beetle dry fly. Who took the fly to Australia, and when, is unknown. Jim Allen wrote: 'My all-round favourite fly is the Red Tag. If I had to pick a single fly from my fly box, then the Red Tag is it. No questions asked. No argument. Number one!' Praise indeed. For Allen the Red Tag is the 'quintessential beetle pattern'. Fellow Australian fly fisherman Ashley Artis described it as 'one of the most successful trout flies ever designed'. He prefers to tie it with a tag of red parrot feather fibres (road kill is the only legal source as the birds are protected in Australia), which he finds are more buoyant and hold their colour better when wet than red wool. Allen uses red duck quill, scarlet floss or a fluorescent tag. Using red feathers for the tag is, as we have seen, a practice that is as old as the pattern.

Australian anglers were soon to discover that the fly could be relied upon to catch brownies and rainbows at any time of the season, either wet or dry, and that it was particularly effective when the fish were feeding on the surface. There are more species of insects in the world than there are animals, and of all insects beetles make up about 40 per cent. They are therefore extremely abundant, particularly in Australia. It is common for trout in Australia to encounter beetles and it is no surprise to find beetles regularly in their stomachs. They seem to love them, and the Red Tag is the quintessential beetle artificial fly. But it is often taken when there are no beetles about or in the fishes' stomachs, so proving its attractiveness. In Australian trout streams, a Red Tag of the right size is a very versatile fly that can be fished dry or wet with surprisingly good results in many different situations.

Because the fly is beetle shaped it is also dynamite when trout are feeding around trees or other structures located in or near the water that beetles inhabit. Fish the Red Tag dry on a long 3–4 lb tippet, especially on bright sunny days when

*Catching a trout of this size and quality should satisfy even the most discerning trout fisherman*

a size 14 or 16 is likely to be most successful. It is also a great searching pattern, but it can equally be fished with confidence to sighted trout. If you get a refusal, simply give the line a slight jerk and generally the trout will come back for a second look, thinking it is alive.

Another well-known Australian angler who favoured the fly was the late David Scholes, who was seen by Noel Jetson to receive a delivery of a gross of Red Tag dry flies tied by the late Dick Wigram. At the time Jetson wondered why he needed so many but he soon knew.

Jim Allen's deer-hair variant has a black deer-hair body, a fluorescent wool tag and a darker or lighter hackle. He ties it on hooks from sizes 6 to 16 while Artis uses sizes 12 to 18.

Rolt also suggested the fly could be tied with a blood-red gamecock or golden plover hackle as a substitute, ribbed with flat or twisted gold. This dressing had killed many grayling and trout for him. He wrote that it was a pattern he relied on when fishing the southern chalk streams. He also recorded G.S. Marryat's version, which had an ibis tag, a blood-red hackle and a body made from a single strand of a blue and yellow macaw tail feather.

Broughton gives a wet version that varies from the dry simply by being tied on a wet fly hook in size 14 or 16. He also mentioned that the original green peacock herl tended to be used on its sister fly, the Orange Tag, with a more sober bronze popular for the Red Tag. It seems sensible to stick with peacock herl for the body because, as Ashley Artis says: 'I believe that peacock herl possesses special colours and characteristics which are very attractive to trout.'

The red tag is easy to tie. It is tied-in first and if left a bit on the long side, it can always be cut back a bit. Then tie-in three strands of peacock herl and wrap along the hook shank to form a beetle-shaped body. Some fly dressers spin the peacock herls together, forming a rope, before winding them on to the hook shank. If wrapping the herls without forming a rope, when you tie-in the herl make sure that the back of the herl (the back of the feather) is facing up. If it is tied in the wrong way, the herl will squash itself when wound on. The end result should be a beetle-shaped body. Finish the fly with eight or ten turns of the hackle to ensure that the fly will float well.

# GOLD-RIBBED HARE'S EAR NYMPH

*Unknown – England*

THE GOLD-RIBBED HARE'S EAR nymph, or GRHE, is another pattern that every fisherman should have in his or her box of nymphs. For such a popular and well-used fly, it is perhaps strange that no one really knows its history. Tom Rosenbauer in *The Orvis Fly-Tying Guide* claims that the fly 'is at least 500 years old'. This suggests that it was being fished at the time when flies were simply flies, and if they were being fished dry they were fished in this way until they were so wet that they sank, when they were fished as wet flies. If Rosenbauer is correct, then it is not surprising that in his book *Fifty Favourite Nymphs*, T. Donald Overfield recorded the originator as 'unknown'. F.M Halford relied heavily on the Hare's Ear around 1885–90, particularly early in the season (although he claimed that it was effective all season long), as did Skues and others.

The pattern had various regional names including the Hare Fleck, or Flax, and Hare's Lug, a lug being a colloquial name for an ear. The dry version that Halford and his contemporaries fished so effectively seems to have sunk quietly into a nymph – and what a nymph.

One of the most informative writers on the early history of the GRHE was Skues, although he wrote that he would like to have known 'who was the

# GOLD-RIBBED HARE'S EAR NYMPH

| | |
|---|---|
| **HOOK:** | Down-eye nymph, size 10–20 |
| **THREAD:** | Primrose, or colour of choice |
| **WEIGHT:** | Round or square lead wire, optional |
| **TAIL:** | Guard hairs from the mask or body of a hare |
| **RIB:** | Fine gold wire, size to suit hook size |
| **BODY:** | Dubbing of mixed fur and guard hairs from the mask of a European hare |
| **THORAX:** | Well picked-out dubbing |
| **WING CASE:** | Section from a turkey or goose secondary feather, mallard primary or from a cock pheasant tail feather |

genius who first conceived its possibilities and how he got at his theory'. He fished the pattern with the 'utmost confidence' when the medium olive dun of spring, with its greenish olive body, was on the water. For him, this was 'the season of the Hare's Ear'. In his book *The Way of a Trout with a Fly*, he described the fly as being dressed 'with a body of dusty grey-brown, ribbed with flat gold and extremely rough'. He found it hard to understand why trout should take it when the natural was an olive green, smooth-bodied fly. Then in *Nymph Fishing for Chalk Stream Trout*, he speculated that trout took it for 'a hatching nymph standing on its partially discarded shuck'.

Darrel Martin maintains that the nymph evolved from a nymphal pattern based on old English dry and wet flies and 'a logical outgrowth of the original dun pattern'. We know that it was tied both with and without wings for very many years. The transition from a hackled dry version to a nymph is easily appreciated. Although Halford knew that it was a killing pattern that, he thought, imitated a hatching nymph, he was so obsessed with fishing the dry fly only, with fly patterns designed to provide an exact imitation of the natural, that even with the addition of wings he could not bring himself to continue to use it as it was not a good enough match of any natural mayfly. He fished it for the last time on 2 June 1902.

I like the pattern because it is a good 'buggy-looking' nymph and it surely owes much of its success to the fact that it represents everything and nothing equally well. It can be tied in any size that takes your fancy, from tiny to big, with or without weight, and can be fished from near the bottom of a river (when well weighted) to the surface film on the end of a well-greased leader. Rubbing a dollop of spit into an unweighted nymph will help it to sink just below the surface. It can also be tied using a range of different dubbings, from natural or dyed hare's fur usually from the mask or face, to squirrel blends and other blends of short, spiky dubbing. Dressings for the fly rarely suggest using the fur from a hare's ear, which raises the question of why the fly is called hare's ear and not hare's mask. The early names Hare Fleck and Hare Flax do not indicate what part of a hare the fur came from. Dictionary definitions of these two words throw no light on the subject.

John Gierach in his book *Good Flies, Favorite Trout Patterns and How They Got That Way*, advocates dubbing that is a blend of darker hair from a European hare's mask mixed with chopped-up guard hairs. The blend should

*A beautiful brown trout that has fallen for the seductive charm of a gold-head nymph*

be a wonderful natural mix of colours – every colour and no colour. He wrote that a GRHE of the right colour when dropped on the ground at your feet would have such a cryptic colouring that you would never find it. Guard hairs from a piece of hare body fur are excellent for the tails. The gold wire rib should be of a diameter to match the hook size. The final element is the wing case, tied over the thorax. Gierach uses different materials depending on hook size: brown wild turkey tail fibres or charcoal grey Canada goose for the smallest hooks and turkey tail for the biggest. Three or four pheasant tail fibres can also be used. Whatever material you use, lap it backwards and forwards enough times to build as big a wing case as you see fit.

T. Donald Overfield gave a very simple dressing using primrose tying silk, three short dark fibres from a hare's ear for the tails, a body made from thinly dubbed fur from the root of a hare's ear and then ribbed with a length of flat gold tinsel. An extra turn or two of dubbing could be added at the thorax which is then picked out with a dubbing needle, to free some of the longer fibres.

# TUP'S INDISPENSABLE

**HOOK:**     Dry fly, size 14–16
**THREAD:**   Yellow
**TAIL:**     Brassy or honey dun cock hackle fibres
**BODY:**     Yellow silk or floss tip, tup's wool mix for the remainder
**HACKLE:**   Brassy or honey dun cock hackle

# TUP'S INDISPENSABLE

*R.S. Austin – England*

THE TUP'S INDISPENSABLE, as it was to become known, was tied as an imitation of a pale watery by R.S. Austin, a professional fly tier from Tiverton in Devon. The actual dressing was a secret for many years, only revealed by G.E.M. Skues following the death of Austin's daughter, who continued to tie the flies professionally after her father died in 1911. It was the dubbing mix used for the body that gave it its distinction and effectiveness. He revealed it in the *Flyfishers' Journal* in 1934. Many attempts were made by other fly dressers to copy the pattern but none was successful because of the secret recipe. Skues was not able to date the recipe more accurately than to about June 1900, based on a handwritten note from Austin describing its first use. It would seem reasonable to assume that Austin had been dressing this pattern for a number of years at the end of the previous century.

Austin had sent Skues the actual fly that he had used to kill a number of big fish at the mouth of the Loman, where it joins the Exe at Tiverton. After Skues had returned the fly, Austin gave him the recipe and sent him a quantity of the magic dubbing so that he could tie some himself. He first tried them on the Wandle in August or September and rose a considerable number of fish, although he hooked few as he was fishing under a tree and had difficulty setting the hook properly. Anyway, he was encouraged enough to give the pattern a trial on the Itchen the following April. He fished only the one fly and caught seven brace of fish.

Skues thought that the fly should have a name and said as much to Austin. Skues mulled over ideas and names such as 'So-and-So's Infallible' and So-and-So's Irresistible' and eventually arrived at Tup's Indispensable. The fly and its name became common knowledge when Skues' basket of fourteen fish was reported in *The Field* the week after their capture.

*A classic view of the Bourne Rivulet made famous in Harry Plunket Greene's book* Where the Bright Waters Meet

The essential part of the dubbing is wool from a tup's, or ram's, scrotum, suitably cleaned and washed. To this was added some pale pinkish, filmy fur from the poll of an English hare and, in the original mixture, cream seal's fur, combings from a lemon yellow spaniel and a small amount of red mohair, to give the mixture the desired dominant colour. Instead of red mohair, Skues used red seal's fur which he believed Austin had used as well. (Although the lamb's wool was not his own idea, Skues himself used some interesting materials for some of his nymphs, including fur from a blue Persian cat dyed in picric acid.) Austin left an undated manuscript for a *Book of Dry-fly Fishing on Exe and Other North Devon Streams* which he may have produced around 1890. This included the dressing for a red spinner, which was to become Tup's Indispensable. The body comprised the tup's wool and enough red mohair – not seal's fur – to produce a pinkish tinge.

To begin with Skues fished the pattern as a dry fly, as was intended. But one day he cast his fly a second time, without drying it, and as it had a soft hackle it sank and a trout turned but missed it. He cast again and hooked the fish. For Skues this was a real discovery and he went on to prove to himself that the fly could be fished wet with success. When wet the colours in the dubbing mixture merged and mixed most seductively and he found it to be a very good imitation of a nymph he found in a trout's mouth. This was to be the start of his long road to becoming the father of nymph fishing. Tied with 'a very short, soft henny hackle' instead of the bright cock's hackle used for the dry version, it became the foundation of his original small range of nymph patterns. He also fished the Tup's semi-submerged, particularly when casting to nymphing fish. Some years later he caught a small trout on a Tup's Indispensable. He killed it and took it with him back to the inn where he was staying. He used his newly discovered marrow spoon to extract the contents of the fish's stomach for analysis.

## PARTRIDGE & ORANGE

| | |
|---|---|
| HOOK: | Down-eye, size 10 or 12, or 16 or 18 |
| THREAD: | Pearsall's Gossamer silk, orange No. 6a |
| BODY: | Orange silk, No. 6a, or the same silk ribbed with about four turns of gold wire or tinsel |
| HACKLE: | Brown mottled (not barred) feather from a partridge's neck or back, two turns only |

# PARTRIDGE & ORANGE

*Unknown – England*

THE PARTRIDGE & ORANGE is one of the most famous North Country spider patterns, often known as soft-hackle flies, particularly in the USA. It is also known as the Orange Partridge. One of the most distinctive features of this traditional pattern is that it must be dressed very lightly and sparsely if its integrity is to be preserved. With a very sparse body and a mere wisp of hackle, getting the proportions correct and the body perfect and in the right position is more challenging than might seem at first, as there can be no extra turns to hide mistakes.

J.W. Hills fished this fly on the River Eden in what was then Cumberland and described it as an old Cumberland pattern, a fancy fly that was fished year-round in the north of England. He claims to have introduced it to the Kennet in about 1912 but did not fish it much, although he thought it was the best sunk pattern on the Test. It became a favourite at Stockbridge and then spread to many other rivers. He also described it as the best imitation of the February red – a specific use – and as a general imitation it killed trout when fished as an imitation of the blue-winged olive nymph. He found it most successful either in large sizes, 2 or 3 (equivalent to a 12 or 10), or very small, 000 (which is a size 17 today).

The fly was tied to represent the *Perlidae* and *Ephermeridae* that trout would have been found feeding on in northern rivers and streams between

*Does line colour matter? This orange line would make many a New Zealand guide wince*

March, the start of the season and the middle of May. The fly would have been fished as one of a team of three or even four flies.

The origins of traditional spider patterns such as the Partridge & Orange can be traced back as far as the first years of the eighteenth century. At the same time as they were being developed, largely in Yorkshire, Stewart in Scotland was developing his own range of Scottish spiders. This was the start of a realization that traditional winged wet flies could be bettered. Spiders represent a very versatile style of tying as they can be fished to represent a wide range of natural flies and different stages of fly life when fished upstream and subsurface in the age-old style.

The body is made from Pearsall's Gossamer silk, of the correct colour, and should end no further along the hook shank than 'half way between the point of the hook and the point of the barb'. This precise position was defined by Harfield N. Edmonds and Norman N. Lee in their book *Brook and River Trouting*, published privately in the second decade of the twentieth century. The silk should also be well waxed with transparent wax, which will make it a shade or two darker than that produced by ordinary waxing. As little as one turn of hackle is often used to produce a really delicate spider pattern.

In *The Way of a Trout with a Fly*, Skues described how to tie this pattern with 'kick', a quality which he said that every wet fly to be fished in rough water should have; with it a fly in the water would appear alive and struggling, without it, it would seem dead. He tied on a partridge hackle and formed the head of the fly before taking the silk back behind the hackle, to finish securing the butt of the hackle. He then wound two turns of hackle and secured the end with a turn of silk. He pulled all the hackle fibres forwards so that he could make a whip finish 'tight up behind the hackle'. This made the fibres stand away from the hook, giving the pattern what he considered its essential 'kick' when fished.

# LUNN'S PARTICULAR

| | |
|---|---|
| **HOOK:** | Snecky Limerick, size 15. Substitutes: Mustad 94840, 94845; Partridge L3A or L3B Capt Hamilton dry fly; Tiemco 5230 or Daiichi 1180, size 14–16 |
| **THREAD:** | Pearsall's Gossamer, shade 13. Substitute: Danville claret 6/0 |
| **TAIL:** | Four fibres from a large Rhode Island hackle |
| **BODY:** | Undyed hackle stalk of a Rhode Island cock hackle |
| **WINGS:** | Two medium blue cock hackle points, tied flat |

# LUNN'S PARTICULAR

*William Lunn – England*

LUNN'S PARTICULAR IS A standard dry fly that has stood the test of time since its birth on the River Test in 1917. It was designed by William Lunn who was head keeper of the Houghton Club's waters of the river from 1 January 1887 until his retirement in 1931. In his biography of Lunn, *River Keeper*, J.W. Hills wrote of Lunn's Particular: 'It kills well when the fish are taking olives, and is marvellously good when they are shy or taking spinners. It succeeds whether floating or sunk. If I had to be limited to one fly, I should choose it.' And in *A Summer on the Test* he described it as 'the best fly in the world' – quite a claim.

Although designed for use in the early spring, it soon became obvious that this was a pattern that was effective throughout the season, and that it represented the spinner of more than one species of olive. Lunn tied it, with spent wings, to imitate a spent olive floating on the water with its wings outstretched. The name of the artificial was transferred to the naturals, which became known as 'particulars'.

William Lunn started tying his own flies in June 1916, at the relatively advanced age of fifty-six, following encouragement from a club member, Edward Power, who was to die three months later. In the spring of 1917 he tried tying a representative of the spinner of the winter dun (*Baetis rhodani*) that is on the water between November and April. On 26 April of that year Arthur N. Gilbey, a very hard fisherman who had been given tuition by G.S. Marryat, according to accounts given by William Lunn's grandson Mick was fishing Park Stream and not having much success. (In *A Summer on the Test*, Hills wrote that Gilbey caught sixty-six trout weighing 136 lb 4 oz during a six-day period in 1906, a catch which he suggested had never been equalled.) He remarked to Lunn: 'The trout are too particular to-day.' Lunn then produced his latest pattern and asked Gilbey to try it. He proceeded to catch three fish with it before the end of a short rise. Gilbey then asked Lunn what the fly was and was told that it was Lunn's Particular. It was destined to become number one in Lunn's list of patterns.

The real humour and cleverness behind this seemingly straightforward name is not revealed by J.W. Hill's no doubt accurate but somewhat dry account. Gilbey was a member of the Gilbey gin-distilling family, and back in 1917 'particular' was a popular term for one's favourite drink. Lunn, whose father had worked in a distillery, had made a clever pun in telling a gin distiller that the fly was his particular. Gilbey was a long-time member of the Houghton Club on the Test and was Secretary for some time. He was also one of the club's most successful fishermen, at least in the eyes of those who would judge success by the numbers of fish caught. Many today would consider him to have been over-zealous in the size of his bags.

According to his grandson Mick, William Lunn was obsessed with inventing and tying flies. He tied his flies in a bedroom at Riverside Cottage at Sheepbridge Shallow on the Test, where he lived. No one was allowed in except by invitation. He created four nymphs and thirty-six dry flies, of which only sixteen were winged. Like that other well-known river keeper, Frank Sawyer, Lunn was blessed with exceptional eyesight and an ability to distinguish minute differences in shades of colour, according to Hills. As Sawyer was to do a few years later, Lunn aimed to produce flies that looked right from the trout's view point.

Lunn has left us a legacy in discovering what a realistic, segmented body for spinners and duns could be made from a stripped and dyed hackle stalk. He was very precise in his demands for exact matches and correct colours of materials for all his flies. He had his feathers dyed by his wife and they had to be the precise shade that he required. Most of his feathers and hackles came from the poultry that he kept, as well as local shoots and the annual cull of moorhens and coots. When fur was needed, he shot his own hares and rabbits.

He had his own special way of tying his Particular. He tied-in the hackle first, as he maintained that it made it easier 'to judge more accurately the other

*Releasing a fine wild brown trout back into the Bourne Rivulet*

proportions of the fly'. He tied-in the wings and hackle stalks at the same time, holding the wings across the shank of the hook while he tied the stalks. He then separated the hackle point wings with figure of eight turns of silk, adjusting the wings so that they were exactly the same length. The hackle stalks were folded back and wound round the body to produce a nice even taper and look. This method meant that the wings could never part company from the hook.

According to the colour chart for Pearsall's Gossamer silks in *Brook and River Trouting*, shade 13 can be described as wine/burgundy red. How accurately the colour was printed in the first place and how much it has faded over the years are, of course, unknown. A modern match can be obtained by using Danville claret 6/0 thread. Mick Lunn wrote that his grandfather only ever used snecky Limerick hooks, which had an offset hook point. Hook size 0 equates to a modern size 15 and odd numbers are not generally available today.

*Adams tied in the style of the original*

# ADAMS

HOOK:      Mustad 94840, size 12 and 14; 94838, size 16–20; Partridge
           E1A, size 12–18; VMC 9288 and 9281, size 12–20
THREAD:    Black, 6/0 or 8/0
TAIL:      Mixed grizzly and brown, or ginger, hackle fibres
BODY:      Natural grey muskrat, or medium grey dubbing
WINGS:     Paired and divided grizzly hackle points or tips
HACKLE:    Mixed grizzly and brown

# ADAMS

*Leonard Halladay – USA*

THE ADAMS IS A deceptively simple dry fly but since its inception in about 1922 it has become one of the top half-dozen dry flies in the USA and many other countries around the world. It is fished with ubiquity and confidence everywhere. An indication of its worldwide popularity is the ease with which so-called Adams grey dubbing can be bought.

Darrel Martin described the Adams as having 'the neutral colour of a caddis and the silhouette of a mayfly' – a simple description that cannot be bettered. He also wrote that 'the true value of the pattern lies in its variegated, but neutral, colors'. History has it that the first Adams was tied by Leonard Halladay, of Mayfield, Michigan, in 1922, and was fished for the first time by Judge Charles E. Adams, from Ohio. Halladay gave a sample to Adams, who fished it on the Boardman River that evening. When he reported on the success that he had had with the pattern, he asked its name. Halladay said 'Adams', as Charles Adams was the first angler to have fished it successfully. Halladay, who was born in 1872, started tying flies in 1917.

Since 1922 a whole host of variants have been produced, with the parachute version probably the most used. In this version, the normal hackle-point wings are replaced with a white calf-tail wing post, around which the hackles are tied, parachute style.

The original dressing may have been as follows:

TAIL:     Two strands of golden pheasant neck feather
BODY:     Grey wool yarn

WINGS:     Grizzly hackle tips tied spent
HACKLE:   Mixed brown and grizzly tied together

This was the dressing given by William F. Blades in his book *Fishing Flies and Fly Tying*, which was first published in 1951. (Another 'original' recipe specified that the wings were tied 'advanced' forward and semi-spent.) Blades was born in Sheffield, had his first fishing lesson on the River Trent and emigrated to the USA at the beginning of the twentieth century, aged twenty-three. He started life as a stonemason and then became a successful building contractor. It was not until he was in his forties that he had time to fish. During the Second World War he taught fly tying in hospitals as therapy for the wounded. He also taught the late Poul Jorgensen how to tie flies.

*Adams tied in the modern style*

*A rainbow trout well hooked in the scissors and ready to be netted*

The main differences between the original and the modern dressing are the golden pheasant tippets for the tail and the fact that the wings were tied spent. If tied with spent wings today, the pattern can be used with success during a spinner fall.

In his book *The Dry Fly, Progress since Halford*, Conrad Voss Bark maintained that the wings were tied upright and a little spread and not too close to the head (eye) of the hook and that the tails were tied long and strong so as to 'lift the hook clear of the water'. The dressing that he published is, effectively, the same as given here.

# COCKY SPINNER

| | |
|---|---|
| HOOK: | Dry fly, size 12 or 14 |
| THREAD: | Hot orange, or red, to choice |
| TAIL: | Medium red cock |
| RIB: | Gold wire |
| BODY: | Two strands of orange, or red, macaw or condor quill |
| HACKLE: | Medium blue cock and medium red cock, both tied with best side to the hook eye |

# COCKY SPINNER

*Major Barton William-Powlett – Australia*

THE COCKY SPINNER REPRESENTS the Australian red spinner *Atalophebia australis*, which was first collected and identified in 1842. Although the Australian red spinner has a relatively restricted distribution, it is an important fly, which trout feed on for most of the season. David Scholes wrote of fishing hatches on the flat rivers in the Australian spring, equivalent to the well-known Duffers' Fortnight when the English mayfly are hatching. The Cocky Spinner was invented in Tasmania by an Englishman, Major Barton William-Powlett, who was a regular visitor to the island for nigh on fifty years, as his wife had family property there. The way that it was designed and tied predated some of Vincent Marinaro's ideas.

William-Powlett recorded in his diary seeing bright orange-bodied spinners in January 1912, and he also noted 'golden brown tinged red spinner(s)'. Dick Wigram thought that the body should be tied using a bright orange condor quill but William-Powlett preferred red. Wigram had more confidence in his orange version. David Scholes described the red spinner as having an abdomen of a rich coppery hue, changing to a 'bright and most conspicuous orange-red' in flight. He first encountered it on the Macquarie River when fishing with Wigram. And it was on the same river that Wigram first fished with William-Powlett, who had fished in Tasmania for many years before Wigram's arrival there.

Dick Wigram described William-Powlett as 'a creative fly tier of great skill' and said, 'His influence on Tasmanian fly dressing in the middle thirties gave local anglers a number of more than useful patterns, some of which are standard for use on both lakes and rivers today [c. 1968].' William-Powlett contributed an article on tying his Buzzwing flies to Dick Wigram's weekly angling column in the Launceston *Weekly Courier* in November 1932.

Major William-Powlett was born in Ryde, Isle of Wight, in 1871. His mother died when he was twelve and his elderly father soon after. He was then separated from his sisters and brought up by the Earl of Portsmouth at Eggesford in Devon, where he learned to hunt, shoot and fish.

After his marriage to Charlotte Reibey, a Devon rector's granddaughter, in 1895, he rented a farmhouse near Abergavenny in Monmouthshire. In 1912 he moved a few miles into Abergavenny and rented a large Edwardian house. That year his wife's favourite great uncle, Tom Reibey III, died childless in Tasmania and may have left her a considerable sum. In 1920 a 99-year trust came to an end, which gave William-Powlett access to the family silver and some property in Lincolnshire. By 1924 his three surviving sons were all launched on military careers. He looked for a smarter house, returning to his and his wife's roots in Devon. Cadhay, in Ottery St Mary, was much grander than he had intended, but seeing his family arms over the fireplace, he gave in to his wife's social ambition and rented it in 1924. He bought it in 1930 after selling the property in Lincolnshire.

He was a member of the Flyfishers' Club, London, from 1932 until 1952, a founder member of the Usk Valley Casting Club and a life member of the British Casting Association. He was a very keen book collector, with a large library of fishing books.

William-Powlett died in April 1953, aged eighty-three, one year before his wife, who had been born in the same year as he was. Emily Charlotte Reibey was a great great granddaughter of one Mary Reibey. Although she would not have appreciated it at the time, Mary Reibey, who was sentenced to death in 1792, aged fourteen and disguised as a boy, for stealing a horse, was to become a major figure in early Australian life. She was born near Bury, Lancashire, on 12 May 1777 and christened Molly Haydock. Her father died in 1779 and her mother also died during Molly's infancy. She was brought up by a grandmother which may have something to do with the fact that she was known as Mary. She spent time in prison – still in disguise and without discovery – before her

*A magnificent gentleman's fishing hut*

sentence was commuted to transportation to Australia for seven years. She left Portsmouth in May 1792 and arrived in Sydney on 7 October.

Although there is no actual proof, it seems that Mary was assigned to the Lieutenant-Governor, Francis Grose, for whom she worked as a nursemaid. Later she went to Sydney where she met Thomas Reibey, a free man. In September 1794, they married. Reibey operated a very successful shipping and trading business, Messrs Reibey and Wills. Their house in Sydney was called Entally House, after a suburb of Calcutta which Thomas Reibey had visited as part of the crew of the *Britannia*, and the same name was used for the house that Thomas Reibey II built in Tasmania at Hadspen near Launceston.

Thomas Reibey died from the delayed effects of sunstroke on 5 April 1811, leaving Mary with seven children and his burgeoning business empire. She ran it most successfully and became a very well-known businesswoman and an astute property developer. She became a director of the Bank of New South Wales and moved in the highest society in Sydney. In March 1820 she and her daughters Celia and Eliza sailed for England, where they travelled widely and visited her relatives. Her sons established businesses in Tasmania and her grandson, Thomas, was Archdeacon of Launceston and Premier of Tasmania. Mary Reibey died on 30 May 1855, aged seventy-eight.

William-Powlett wrote to Wigram about his Buzzwing flies, which he designed to be very durable by turning the silk 'through all the hackles making it impossible for them to come undone':

*The 'buzzwing' method is quite an easy one and the result is a very hard-wearing fly which floats very lightly and naturally on the water and which gives no trouble to make it 'cock'. It will fish wet, too. I often used the same fly for both methods alternately. After killing a fish the fly may want smoothing out; then a few flicks and it is dry and floating again.*

*This method results in a specially buoyant fly that sits with body and legs lightly on the water. They are the most durable flies made and are not difficult to tie.*

*The wings are formed with a hackle or hackles mixed, or with a slab of feather in the midst of a hackle to obtain a particular colouring to match the natural. If a slab of feather is used, I roll it up and tie it in to stand right on top of the hook. Only a small piece is needed. In one pattern of mine, I split this rolled-up feather after it has been tied in and splay it out on either side of the body and then turn on the hackles so that it is in the midst of them.*

*Tails help a fly to float well. A trout can't count, so tie in three or four stiff fibres – or more in a big fly – from a cock's spade feather. Proceed as usual up to the point where the body is finished. Be careful to leave plenty of room to turn on the wing-hackle and legs.*

*Select suitable hackles for the above. The hackle-fibre wings should be slightly longer in fibre than a slab feather wing would be. The tips are invisible and help to give buoyancy.*

*Tie in the wing-hackle by the butt. Wind it tailwards, secure the point and take a turn behind the hackles close up so as to press them forward, then turn the silk through the hackle to the neck and make a half-hitch on the neck. Press the hackles with your fingernails on the quill back towards the tail. This presses the coils as close as possible. Now remove the hook from the vice and replace it with the bend and point uppermost. This will make further operations easy.*

*Part the hackle fibres by stroking them downwards on either side of the body. Take the silk which is hanging at the neck – this silk should be the colour that is required for the underpart of the thorax which you are about to dress – and turn it from the neck over the hackle to close behind the hackle, round the body and cross the first lap of silk back to the neck. This forms an 'X' of silk on the thorax over the turns of hackle. Take a turn around the neck, then a turn over the first lap of silk, and leave the silk hanging taut, close behind the wing-hackle on the far side. No fibres of hackle should be lying much below or, as the hook lies now, above, the level of the body. If there are any, pluck them off rather than cutting them.*

*The hackle should now be evenly parted and the lowest fibres at right angles to the body of the fly, and all inclined over the head. If the hackles have been tied in best-side tailwards, which is often possible, this effect is always produced and is desirable because the fibres are then not likely to engage under the bend of the hook. Tying in the hackle inside-out often makes a better imitation and except in red hackles, does not alter the appearance. Besides, we cannot be sure whether trout will inspect our fly from before or behind.*

*One or more extra wing-hackle may be added, the other being a soft natural hackle or a cock hackle dyed to give a desired tint when mixed with a natural. The natural cock hackle must be turned on last, through and on each side of the others, and be the longest in fibre.*

*Select a hackle suitable for the legs. If it is a small fly – No. 1 and less – three or four turns are sufficient and those should be close up behind the wings. The fibres should be as short as possible. It need not be a high quality hackle as the wings ought to be – that is, a bright, glassy hackle from an old bird. In big long-bodied flies, it is advisable to use two leg-hackles or spread them out more along the body to help support it in the water.*

*Turn the silk back through the coils of hackle, secure the point, and from your side take the silk back over the thorax to the neck. With whip finish, or half hitches, make off and do form the head. Varnish.*

The resulting fly will sit naturally close to the surface of the river, on its legs (hackle) and body, not legs and tail. It will have a good silhouette without the 'dense bumble of hackle tied in for legs' but with 'a thorax under the fly in the right place and the right colour making the fly look extremely natural'. The long hackles used for the wing will be 'easy to see, and yet are transparent like the natural, reflecting light and tinting according to background'. He wrote that these patterns sit lightly on the water which he maintained was one of their chief attractions, particularly to difficult trout. He realized the importance of the thorax on artificial flies, like Marinaro, but he did not move it back along the hook shank as Marinaro did in his thorax flies. Marinaro wrote in 1950 in his book *A Modern Dry Fly Code*, 'I do not discount the practicality of a wing formed by hackle only, tied buzz fashion.'

# GRAY WULFF

*Lee Wulff – USA*

LEE WULFF STARTED DEVELOPING his new pattern, which was to become known as the Gray Wulff, in 1929 to imitate the upwing mayflies on the rivers that he fished, including the Hendrickson on the Beaverkill in the spring and the large, grey-coloured drakes found on the Ausable River at Wilmington, New York State. He tied it 'in rebellion against the typical British-type dry flies'. Although he could see that these slender flies were attractive – certainly to the angler's eye – he felt that a hungry trout would be more likely to rise for a pattern that offered the prospect of a good mouthful such as the big *Isonychia* duns and *Ephemera* spinners. The greyish flies were to be found during most of the summer and were heavy bodied. Wulff used bucktail to give the tail of his artificial enough buoyancy to float the big, bulky body. Bucktail is strong as well as buoyant. The heavy body was tied using grey angora wool. The size also imitated the bulky body of the main terrestrials that fell on to the water. The resulting fly was very durable as well as buoyant. Lee Wulff claims that this was the first ever use of animal hair on a dry fly.

Wulff's friend and fishing companion Dan Bailey was responsible for the name of the Gray Wulff. Originally Wulff called it the Ausable Gray but Bailey insisted that it be called the Gray Wulff – a very prescient decision.

The fly was introduced to the River Test by the American ambassador, Lewis Douglas, in the early 1950s at Stockbridge. He was the only American ever to be elected a member of the Houghton Club in his own right. The Gray Wulff has since become the fly of choice on most English rivers during the mayfly (*E. Danica*) hatch of late May and early June.

## GRAY WULFF

| | |
|---|---|
| **HOOK:** | Mustad 94845 or 7957b, size 10–18 |
| **THREAD:** | Grey |
| **TAIL:** | Brown bucktail |
| **BODY:** | Grey angora yarn |
| **WING:** | Brown bucktail |
| **HACKLE:** | Two long, dyed, blue dun saddle hackles |

Wulff used the fly first on the Esopus, then the Beaverkill and afterwards on the Ausable. He caught fifty-one fish on the first Gray Wulff that he fished on the Salmon River, near Malone in New York State when fishing with Dan Bailey. It was tied on a size 10 hook which was the size he used most of the time. He had to re-grease it after every fifth or sixth fish.

Lee Wulff was born in 1906, in Valdez, Alaska, where he grew up. He was another fly fisherman who started tying flies when he was young, aged thirteen, having started fishing when he was ten. He then moved to New York with his parents and, in 1920, to California. He moved to Louisville, Kentucky, in 1930 around the same time that he was developing his Wulff pattern. He left his job and returned to fish on the Ausable River at the end of the season and was able to confirm that the fly was still a good imitation of the late-hatching grey drakes.

*The mayfly provides for many the cream of English trout fishing often referred to somewhat contemptuously as Duffers' Fortnight*

Some authorities state quite categorically that the wing should not be split. Wulff wrote that the wing was split 'so they are set in the right position' by winding the tying thread between and around the base of the two wings, with plenty of wraps of thread in front of the wings to make them stand up straight. Although to begin with he tied his wings upright, when he was imitating mayflies, he admitted to having seen tyings with wings slanted forwards as well as back. He also tried a single wing, either upright or with a rearward slant, and he found it to be just as successful as the split-wing version. But during the Depression, when he was working as a freelance artist in New York and money was hard to come by, he tied his flies the way that his customers wanted them, with split wings, as they felt that they were getting more value for their money. But he did feel that the single wing was a better imitation, as all natural upwing flies float with their wings together. Divided wings were more visible to the angler and gave the fly 'better flotation'. When fishing fast water he would tie his flies with as many as three hackles to give them extra buoyancy. Wulff was very happy to vary his tyings and choice and selection of materials, using a range of density of materials and colour variations. This fits in well with his statement that his Wulff patterns were a category of flies and not inflexible patterns that must never be varied.

All through his tying instructions he stressed the importance of using plenty of varnish, or head cement, to hold and lock everything in place on the hook shank. He applied varnish to the first wraps of tying thread to produce a good, firm base so that the rest of the materials would not slip round the hook. He applied varnish after he had tied-in the tail, which also helped to hold the wool body in place. All this helped produce tough, durable, hard-working flies. More varnish, or lacquer, was applied to the base of the wing or wings, if they were split. The head cement should still be wet when tying the hackles. He brought one back between the wings, and wrapped it round the shank close to the wings until he was left with just enough hackle to bring it forward again between the wings and tie-down with the second hackle, which was wrapped in front of the wings. Then both hackle tips were tied-down with tying thread and a neat head tied to finish the fly. And do not forget to varnish the head.

Variations of the original Gray Wulff include the White Wulff, to represent the coffin fly – the spent stage of the green drake; the Royal Wulff, which he claimed turned the Royal Coachman (which was difficult to keep afloat) into 'a hell of a fly'; the Grizzly Wulff; the Black Wulff, developed independently by both Dan Bailey and Ray Bergman; the Brown Wulff, and the Blonde Wulff. The last four variations he developed with his old friend and early fishing companion Dan Bailey who started his fly shop in Montana in 1958. Wulff tied the White Wulff both conventionally and in a spent form with no hackle to match the spinner of the coffin fly. The White Wulff is tied with a cream-coloured angora body and badger hackles.

Depending on hook size and colour of materials used, a Wulff pattern can be fished and presented to represent almost any type of natural fly that a hungry trout is likely to see. It is a truly versatile and durable pattern.

## HUMPY

| | |
|---|---|
| **HOOK:** | Mustad 7957B, 94840; Partridge E1A orL3A or equivalent dry fly, size 10–18 |
| **THREAD:** | Black, red, yellow or green, for body colour |
| **TAIL:** | Moose or elk body hair |
| **BODY:** | Tying thread or floss |
| **OVERBODY:** | Moose or elk hair |
| **WING:** | Tips of moose or elk hair overbody, upright and divided |
| **HACKLE:** | Two black or brown or brown and grizzly mixed |

# HUMPY

*Uncertain – USA*

THE HUMPY IS A first-rate, versatile searching pattern that is very buoyant, which makes it well suited to fast, rough waters. The pattern can be tied in many different colours, to represent a wide range of insects and bugs such as adult caddis, mayflies, beetles and even grasshoppers. It can represent anything that a trout wants to eat. It is known sometimes as the Goofus Bug in the USA. A 1981 advertisement for Dan Bailey's flies is illustrated with twelve flies, one of which is a Goofus Bug or Improved Humpy. In the same magazine, *Fly Fisherman*, for May 1993, an article by Sylvester Nemes also refers to the Goofus Bug.

Lee Wulff wrote that the Humpy 'came out of the West' at about the same time that he was developing his Gray Wulff in 1929–30. It is generally accepted that the name Humpy (which is associated with Wyoming), derives from the humped body, but what is not known is who its inventor was. It may originate from near Jackson Hole, Wyoming, or from a fly tier in San Francisco, Jack Horner, who used a folded deer-hair body with the tips of the hair forming wings on his Horner's Deer Hair fly in the mid-1930s; this fly is sometimes referred to as the Little Jack Horner. According to Craig Mathews and John Juracek, the Goofus Bug, which they claim was perfected by Pat and Sig Barnes, owners of a tackle shop in West Yellowstone, is a close relative of the Horner Deer Hair. An article, 'The Evolution of the Humpy' in *Fly Tyer* magazine, by Joseph 'Boots' Allen, suggested that Horner got the inspiration for his fly from a Canadian pattern, the Tom Thumb. This is a simple 'dry fly for all seasons' tied

*Turbulent water is always full of oxygen and the turbulence makes it harder for fish to see approaching danger*

with deer hair for its tail, body and wing. It has no hackle. Allen also wrote that Pat and Sig Barnes started tying the Goofus Bug, after witnessing the effectiveness of Horner's Deer Hair at the hands of a visiting angler from California in 1943. At the end of the 1940s, Allen's grandfather, Leonard 'Boots' Allen, a fly tier and outfitter in Jackson Hole, started tying a variation of both the Goofus Bug and Horner's Deer Hair which became known as the Humpy. 'Boots' Allen's fly soon became a standard pattern in the fly boxes of anglers all over

Wyoming and Idaho. He tied them with mule deer hair taken from the neck, face and hindquarters, with a heavy grizzle hackle – often eight to twelve turns – and in large sizes a size 8 was standard and never smaller than a size 10.

Whoever is responsible for the fly came up with a remarkably successful and versatile pattern that is extremely buoyant and very tough too. Dan Bailey's catalogue described them as floating 'even better than the Wulff patterns, though they are slightly less desirable.' In his article, Joseph 'Boots' Allen quoted Bruce Staples as having said: 'The saga of the Humpy's true origin goes on and will probably remain a source of friendly discussion for years to come.'

Jack Dennis, who had a fly tying shop in Jackson, Wyoming, produced many thousands of Humpies in the 1970s. He made some subtle changes to the Allen version including using elk or moose hair for the tail, as the original deer hair was not very durable, and elk and different deer hairs for the body to add even more buoyancy. Jay and Kathy Buuchner, who tied for Dennis in the 1970s, also made changes including using elk and moose hair and they found that using different coloured tying thread could represent specific insects better.

The Humpy is not an easy fly to tie. The key to tying it successfully is, as with so many patterns, getting the proportions right and the tier's ability to handle and manipulate the materials properly. You need to measure correctly the length of hairs used for the tail and the overbody/wing hair as well. Once the tail has been tied to just the right length, you can measure the overbody/wing hair so that it is the same length as the hook shank and the tail combined. Get the tail right and everything else will follow correctly.

When tied in fluorescent green it makes a good imitation for a New Zealand beetle and no doubt other beetles too. The Humpy can be fished as a mayfly, caddis or adult stone fly and can even represent small terrestrials.

# MUDDLER

| | |
|---|---|
| **HOOK:** | Size 2–14 3X or 4X long streamer |
| **WEIGHT:** | Lead wire, optional |
| **THREAD:** | Black 6/0 |
| **TAIL:** | Two sections of turkey tail feather, mottled |
| **BODY:** | Flat gold tinsel |
| **UNDERWING:** | Fox squirrel tail or brown bucktail |
| **OVERWING:** | Mottled turkey tail feather sections, paired |
| **COLLAR:** | Tips of head deer hair |
| **HEAD:** | Deer hair, flared and trimmed to a bullet shape |

# MUDDLER

*Don Gapen – USA*

THE MUDDLER FLY WAS created by Don Gapen, in 1937, when he was fishing the Nipigon River in Ontario, Canada, which was famous for its trophy brook trout. He ran the first float-plane fly-in fishing and guiding business in northern Ontario. He created the Muddler to represent the sculpin minnow, which is an important part of the diet of trout – especially big trout – although it is a good imitation of many forms of trout food. It is a fly which can be fished dry, wet, semi-submerged and deep as a darting sculpin or minnow, when tied weighted. The shaped deer hair head imitates the shape of a small baitfish very well, as well as creating a considerable disturbance in the water or on the surface if being fished dry.

Tie it weighted to fish deep, near the bottom to imitate bottom-hugging baitfish. Let it tumble along the bottom, giving it the occasional twitch as though it is trying to swim properly on an even keel. When tied unweighted and fished dry, cast one near the banks to imitate grasshoppers and other terrestrials that have fallen on to the water. Although it can be tied in large sizes, this is not necessary and smaller sizes will cast that much more easily. Also, in smaller sizes it is a good representation of chunky nymphs such as those of stoneflies.

My researches suggest that Don Gapen tied his original Muddler with the deer hair head on the sparse side and spun fairly loosely. John Geirach, in *Good Flies*, quotes a guide on the Minipi River in Labrador as saying that the head should be loose – and fat and round – so that it can be squeezed wet to stop it floating.

*A genuine Muddler tied by Don Gapen*

Dave Hughes maintains that 'the Muddler is mandatory in any exploratory fly box'. With a recommendation like that, any angler who fishes a range of different waters should ensure that they have some. Many anglers have Dan Bailey to thank for making this pattern available commercially.

# WIGRAM'S BROWN OR POT SCRUBBER NYMPH

*Dick Wigram – Australia*

AN ENGLISHMAN, RICHARD HENRY Wigram, played an important role in the development of fly fishing in Australia, particularly in Tasmania. He is probably best known for his Brown or Pot Scrubber nymph. This fly killed fish all over Australia and New Zealand, and Wigram wrote that many English anglers had been converted to it after he had used it to catch difficult trout on the River Colne at Bibury and 'a great many trout and grayling in both the Bristol and Hampshire Avons and the Test on small sizes of this fly' in the mid-1950s when he lived in England for a year. Later he wrote that a friend had used it with success in the USA.

    Wigram was born in England on 25 February 1903, and as a teenager he had fished on the Itchen at Abbotts Barton, where Skues fished. Skues wrote about him in an article, 'The Rising Generation', in the *Journal of the Flyfisher's Club* in 1918: 'Young Dick – another fourteen-year-old – is going to be a mighty

# WIGRAM'S BROWN OR
# POT SCRUBBER NYMPH

HOOK:     Down-eye, wide gape nymph, size 10–14

THREAD:    Brown or black, fine

WEIGHT:    Copper wire (optional)

TAIL:     A few strands from a dark Rhode Island red hackle, tied short

RIB:     Strip of flat copper from a copper pot scrubber, three or four turns depending on hook size, or flat copper strip or copper-colour tinsel, as available

BODY:    Equal quantities of seal's fur and unspun white wool, dyed a rather red dark chocolate brown colour

THORAX:   As body, but twice as thick

HEAD:    An extra pinch of the seal's fur/wool mix

angler before the Lord. Already he ties trout flies with quite a professional touch in them.' He was given his first fly rod, an old greenheart, when he was seven, and slept with it at the foot of his bed and the reel under his pillow. His uncle took him to fish the Itchen with Skues one May day. Wigram fished with 'a little nine-foot American split cane [rod]'. He caught a fish – 'a good two pounds' – on a hackled alder of his own tying. Later he caught another on a yellow dun, tied by Skues, but he fell into a hole while playing the fish which he lost in a patch of weed. Skues recorded that his regret 'is that I shall not be here to see how he shapes when in his prime'.

When he was twenty-one, Dick Wigram and his brother John emigrated to Tasmania. His first fishing in Australia was in New South Wales, and for a few weeks on the Kiewa River in Victoria. He worked as a professional fly tier in Tasmania and although he had to tie at least eighteen flies an hour to make a profit, he still managed to fish almost every day, particularly on the Macquarie River, his favourite, and the South Esk. He had started tying his own flies aged twelve when he did not have enough pocket money to buy commercially tied flies.

He returned to England in 1946, after learning of the death of a relative, in the hope of claiming a share of the estate. Once in England he discovered that he had been left nothing and his finances were so bad that he could not afford to return to Tasmania until a friend sent him the funds for his return passage. Then in 1955, he and his second wife, Sheelah, decided to retire to England, where he rented a cottage on the Wiltshire Avon. He lived in England for two years and tied flies for Ogden Smiths and Farlows 'who ordered three or four hundred dozen at a time', and other English companies. He fished with Frank Sawyer a number of times during this stay and on his subsequent return to Tasmania took with him information on how Sawyer tied and fished his nymphs. On the ship back to Australia, he met Ken Ross and his wife, Jean, and together they opened a tackle shop in Tasmania called Wigram and Ross. The venture was financed by Jean Ross, who had private funds, although it nearly bankrupted her.

Wigram lived in fairly straitened circumstances for most of his life, although his last years were more comfortable as a local businessman provided him with a home and car. He wrote a number of books between 1938 and 1953, contributed regular fishing columns to local newspapers and wrote many magazine articles, both in Australia and England. He died after a car accident in April 1971. His last work, *The Fly*, was published posthumously in 2002 after the manuscript had been discovered two years earlier in Victoria.

Wigram was an exceptional angler and enjoyed nymph fishing, which he described as a 'most fascinating method' that for him, had 'proved very much easier than the usual methods of wet and dry fly'. In the 1930s nymph fishing in Tasmania was still not very popular although, in Wigram's opinion, the rivers were very suitable. He sought suggestion in his artificial nymph patterns rather than exact imitation. He had a list of six essential nymphs which he stated must be 'correct in colour and shape', as these were the patterns that caught the big fish, whereas the 'near enough' patterns would, in his opinion, catch only the smaller trout. He encouraged anglers to spend time watching nymphs when hatching to learn how they swam and moved.

He was responsible for developing Tasmania's most famous nymph – and what he described as his most effective fish-getter – between 1931 and 1935. Roy Dean, who met him in 1934 and fished with him regularly, claimed that he may have been one of the first to fish Wigram's Brown or Pot Scrubber nymph in the spring of 1936. It is possible that he based it on a brown nymph that found its way from England to Tasmania, possibly through his friend from Devon, Major Barton William-Powlett, who visited Tasmania many times during the first half of the twentieth century and had a big influence on local fly tiers and the development of Tasmanian fly patterns.

Wigram's nymph became known as the Pot Scrubber because of the inclusion of a strand of flat copper from a copper pot scrubber instead of the original rib of fine gold wire. As a brown nymph, the body was well tapered and fully ribbed, and there was no thorax. Another early version had two turns of hackle at the head to represent legs. Tails on early versions were three feather fibres with the middle one separated from the other two. The thorax was added when Wigram started to rib the abdomen only with the flat copper. A fishing friend, Frank Wadley, is reputed to have tied a giant nymph, ribbed with a strip of copper from a copper pot scrubber, which he called a pot scrubber nymph. The story goes that Wigram immediately saw the commercial value of this name and added the pot scrubber rib to his own Brown nymph, which then became known as Wigram's Pot Scrubber.

He tied it with a mixture of seal's fur and wool, as he felt that the slightest movement of a fur-bodied fly would cause the ends of the fur fibres to move in

*It is all too easy to lose a fish when you try to net it*

a lifelike way. He mixed wool with fur as it helped bind the fur together and made it more secure when dubbed on a hook. What was crucial to the success of the fly was dyeing equal quantities of seal's fur and unspun white wool (in a diary he wrote 'rather more fur than wool') to exactly the right shade, which he described as a 'rather red chocolate colour'. He used a now obsolete brand of dye called Dolly Dye and mixed together five packets of nigger [sic] brown, half a packet of pillar box red and one third of a teaspoon of black, with a tablespoon of vinegar in half a pint of water. He described the strands, when dry and held up to the light, as showing a 'definite reddish tint, but without the strong light background, it should look a darkish chocolate brown'. The original dressing was tied with either brown or black gossamer silk, with a dozen strands from a dark hackle of a Rhode Island red for a short tail, the dyed seal's fur/wool mix for the abdomen and thorax (with the thorax twice as thick as the body) and a rib of flat copper wire from a pot scrubber. As copper pot scrubbers are, apparently, no longer available, copper strip or flat copper-coloured tinsel of a suitable size will have to be used instead. Wigram finished the fly with an extra pinch of the fur/wool mix at the head.

Wigram preferred down-eye hooks made from good heavy wire, with a wide gape, after the style of the Captain Hamilton hook. This would suggest that he did not add weight to his dressings but relied on the weight of the hook to sink the nymph. Towards the end of his life he tied all his nymphs weighted with copper wire – no doubt influenced by Frank Sawyer – and he added it to his famous Brown or Pot Scrubber nymph.

# GRIFFITH'S GNAT

*George Griffith – USA*

GEORGE GRIFFITH, OF GRAYLING, Michigan, was a founder of Trout Unlimited. He chaired the inaugural meeting of a group of fifteen conservation-minded anglers at his home on 18 July 1959, on the banks of the Au Sable River, where he had a cabin called the Barbless Hook. This was at a time when state policy favoured stocked trout over wild trout and the Au Sable was threatened by logging operations, pollution and development on its banks and across its watershed. He was president of the TU from 1961 to 1964. He died in 1998 aged ninety-seven.

The fly that carries his name, Griffith's Gnat, is a first-class representation of the many midge larvae and pupae that are to be found in highly alkaline rivers such as the Au Sable, particularly when it is fished in the surface film in imitation of a hatching midge that is still tangled up in its pupal shuck or skin. It will also imitate small clumps of mating midges. How big a clump depends on the size of hook being used.

Although this simple fly was developed in Michigan, Ernest Schwiebert endorsed its success on western rivers when he fished it with great success in Yellowstone Park. Its development probably dates back to the 1930s and it may have been known as the Badger Gnat. The Griffith's Gnat is also known as the Grey Palmer in Slovenia.

One point to bear in mind when tying and fishing this fly is the difference

## GRIFFITH'S GNAT

HOOK:      Mustad 94840 or equivalent standard dry fly, size 12–26
THREAD:  Gudebrod black 8/0 or 10/0
BODY:      Peacock herl
HACKLE:  Grizzly, palmered through body

in quality of modern hackles from those of the period when this fly was developed, mainly the stiffness of today's genetic hackles, particularly in sizes suitable for tiny hooks. This may mean that the fly will float *on* the surface rather than *in* the surface film. If you do not have any soft hackles, it could help to grease only the top of the fly, with no grease underneath, to encourage it to sit lower in the water.

Although it is a simple fly, it is important to tie it with the right materials and, particularly in very small sizes, to select the correct size of peacock herl for the body and hackle. Darrel Martin recommended using the long, fine herls from the base of a peacock sword feather for hook sizes 20 and smaller so that they do not choke the hook gape. The hackle should have fibres that are equal in length to the gape of the hook. Between four and eight turns will be required, depending on hook size. To produce a fly of a different shade, hackles other than grizzly can be used.

## MATONA

| | |
|---|---|
| **HOOK:** | Mustad 36665A streamer hook, size 4 |
| **THREAD:** | Bright red |
| **BODY:** | None (bare hook shank) |
| **WING:** | Two pairs of yellow-dyed grizzly cock feathers |
| **COLLAR:** | One yellow-dyed grizzly cock feather |

# MATONA

*Pepe Navas – Argentina*

THE MATONA WAS ONE of the first flies that Pepe Navas ever tied. In 1937 he was working in the new Alumine police station, and in the afternoons he concentrated on fishing, mostly for brook trout, using spoons and sometimes lures. But when March came everything changed and the fish rejected everything that he threw at them. He had some basic fly-fishing tackle, but no flies – and for fly-tying materials, he had nothing.

He opened an old pillow and found a bunch of nice-looking small partridge feathers, which he tied to an ordinary hook – no body, no tail, nothing but two single feathers tied on back to back. Sadly, this basic fly was no more attractive to the local brook trout than his spinners; he caught nothing. But things did change the next season when he hooked his first rainbows at the Alumine and Quillen river junction using his own creations. It helped that he had bought some more fly-fishing tackle. Later, Jorge Donovan told him that the equipment that he was trying to use was extremely unbalanced; his rod was too heavy and slow and the line too light.

One day two British anglers came to fish and one of them gave him some flies, including an American red and black streamer that was a real killer – until he broke the hook on a bad cast. He undressed it and carefully tried to reproduce the pattern on another hook. From that moment he was enthusiastic about red as a colour for flies. But when he tried to buy some red feathers he failed, as the stock of fly-tying materials was very limited. The only thing to do was to dye feathers himself.

However, the closest dye he could get to red was orange. He ignored it then, but that colour is, in his opinion now, one of the most effective in fishing. He took some feathers from an *avutarda* (a type of goose) and dyed them; the result was a beautiful orange and black barred feather. He then tied just two feathers, with the concave side pointing out, which in his opinion gives more life to the pattern, to his hook.

Later, he met a married couple from Scotland on the river. When he told the woman that he tied all his flies, she asked him to repair some damaged ones and make a black and yellow pattern, with no further guidance on size, type or shape. This, she said, was a very effective colour combination in Scotland. He tied a sort of streamer by wrapping a soft yellow hackle over the shank and used two short black chicken feathers for the main wing. The woman caught some very nice trout, including browns weighing over 2 kg. Navas was most impressed, and he started developing his own yellow-black streamer. He asked a friend, a Mr Blaquier, to bring him some Sussex chickens from Pigue, Buenos Aires, and received a cage of noisy chickens some days later!

He set about dyeing some of these new feathers and the result was a beautiful black and yellow feather with irregular bars. He tied on a size 4 streamer hook with the feather tips pointing out again. Thus his Matona was born without him realizing it. When he started to field test it, the results were amazing. The trout took this pattern really hard and he also realized that it encouraged the big ones to rise for it. The average size of fish caught was noticeably larger. He also compared his catches with those of his companions, and his were larger on average. This had never happened to him before.

The man credited with naming the Matona fly was a Federico Roberto Bennet, a member of a famous fishing club, Norysur, on the Meliquina Lake, to the north of Bariloche. Navas worked at the club (presumably as an angling guide) for a long time. The year after Navas first made the then-unnamed Matona, Mr Bennet came to Quillen again and holding the pattern high in his hand he announced: '*Es una mátona barbara*' ('It is an amazing *mátona*'). *Mátona* could be translated as 'killer'.

Navas thinks that his pattern is so successful because the colour is very similar to a baby perch, a very abundant species on the eastern side of Patagonia. Also, the *bagres*, or catfish, are not dark in those waters: they show some dirty yellow traces along the body and their bodies are more slender than regular catfish. This is another good reason for the large trout to attack, whereas the small and medium-sized fish normally feed on nymphs, crustaceans and all sorts of bugs. On the other hand, the large fish look for more consistent food sources, such as crayfish, crabs, smaller trout, perch and catfish.

Navas has also used the Matona to catch landlocked salmon. Fishing with friends using traditional salmon flies, he had the chance to prove that a simple fly could be much more efficient than these regular salmon patterns.

# NYMBEET

| | |
|---|---|
| **HOOK:** | Down-eye wide gape, size 12–18 |
| **THREAD:** | Black 3/0, 6/0 for small sizes |
| **TAIL:** | Three or four strands from a natural black cock hackle |
| **BACK OR WING CASE:** | Slip cut from a crow wing feather, wide enough to double over, glossy-side exposed |
| **BODY:** | Length of nylon from a white pot scrubber, wrapped over tying thread |
| **LEGS:** | One turn only soft black cock hackle |

# NYMBEET

*Stuart Napier – Australia*

BEFORE THE DAYS OF automatic dishwashers, going fishing after a meal would have been one way of getting out of helping with the washing up. But some fly fishermen were obviously familiar with the equipment needed to clean pots and pans, as is demonstrated by the strips of material from both copper and nylon pot or pan scourers that have been used to tie very successful nymphs in Australia. Stuart Napier's use of material from a nylon pot scrubber in his Nymbeet pattern is most likely to have been one of the very first uses of a synthetic material in tying a fly.

He farmed near St Mary's in north-eastern Tasmania and had exclusive access to the Break O'Day River. He created the pattern between the late 1940s and early to mid-1950s and he christened it Nymbeet because it was half nymph and half beetle. His friends were certainly fishing with this fly, or with Napier when he was using it, in 1955. It was first publicized by Napier's friend David Scholes in the latter's book *Fly-fisher in Tasmania* (published in 1961) and then in 2000, in his book *The Enchanting Break O'Day*, Scholes described the first fish that he had seen seduced by a Nymbeet, on 21 October 1956. It was 'an old friend' of Napier's, heavily spotted, and turned the scales at 5 lb – quite a fish from 'a charming little stream'. In *Lifelong Pleasure: Seventy Years of Fly Fishing*, John Brookes wrote that Stuart Napier, with whom he fished often, had just invented the Nymbeet in 1955. It fell out of fashion for many years for no good reason, but people are starting to realize again what a great fly it is.

Dick Wigram described the Nymbeet as a 'great fly made by an angler with years of fishing knowledge behind him, a fly that can confidently be put to difficult trout.'

Like copper scourers, white nylon ones are relatively difficult to find, although you can find them in other colours in discount shops and on market stalls. It is not known if Napier used new scrubbers or old ones that were about to be discarded. Various descriptions of the Nymbeet described it as having a greyish-coloured body suggesting a used scrubber, but the grey colour may well have been the black tying thread showing through the translucent white nylon of a new or nearly new one. Rick Keam met Napier after he had retired from farming and fished occasionally with Keam's father. Napier told him: 'Scholes didn't get my Nymbeet right. He said the stuff I used was grey – it wasn't grey, it was a sort of clearish white. And he reckoned I used two dozen strands from a crow's wing for the back. What're you supposed to do? Count 'em out with a pin or something? All you need is a good bunch.' Rick Keam was also surprised to be told that it was a good small stream fly as Scholes had left everyone with the impression that it was mainly a lake fly, although he first saw it being fished on a river.

It should be dressed sparsely to allow it to sink quickly. I have read suggestions that a small gap should be left between each wrap of the pot scrubber to increase the appearance of segmentation. This can be difficult to achieve on small hooks. If the flat nylon material from a pot scrubber is too wide, try splitting it in half, or use 10 or 12 lb nylon mono or clear Vinyl Rib. The slip of crow feather for the back, or wing case, should be wide enough so that when folded in half and pulled forwards over the back of the fly it will extend nearly halfway down the side of the body. The folded slip means that the glossy side can be used on the outside. The fibres used for the tail should be about the same length as the hook shank.

Although it can be difficult to convert hook sizes from forty or fifty years ago to their modern equivalents – there were inconsistencies between Redditch hook makers then as there are differences today between Japanese and Norwegian hooks – and conversion charts are included in some books, this is a fly that should be tied on small hooks.

# BEACON BEIGE

*Peter Deane – England*

'MAY I PLEASE WARN you, again and again, that an overdressed Beacon Beige is as unpleasant to be with as an overdressed woman.' So wrote Conrad Voss Bark in *Conrad Voss Bark on Flyfishing*.

I was introduced to the Beacon Beige when fishing the Kennet near Axford with a friend who has a rod on a delightful upper stretch of this river. He discovered the fly in a catalogue of the late Dermot Wilson, and has had such outstanding success with it over the last thirty years that if he had to use just one dry fly this would be the one – in a range of sizes, of course. This pattern has proved to be an excellent generic dry fly and will always be associated with the professional fly tier Peter Deane, who claimed to have tied more of this pattern than all others put together. It has strong army connections, from its inception onwards.

Captain Wills, a member of the Wills tobacco and cigarette family, was home on leave from France during the First World War in 1917, and he designed a fly he called the Beige and had instant success with it. He then gave the pattern to Fred Tout, a professional fly tier in Dulverton, to tie as and when he received orders for it and it soon found popularity in Devon around Dulverton.

In March 1948 Peter Deane decided to start a fly-tying business, although he had never tied a fly in his life and was not a fly fisherman. He had, however, come by a copy of Burrard's *Fly Tying in Principle and Practice*. Confined as he was to a wheelchair, his prospects of earning a living at that time must have

## BEACON BEIGE

| | |
|---|---|
| **HOOK:** | Dry fly, down eye, wide gape, size 12–18 |
| **THREAD:** | Yellow micro |
| **TAIL:** | Four fibres from a Plymouth rock or grizzle cock |
| **BODY:** | Stripped peacock quill from the eye feather, with clearly defined markings |
| **HACKLE:** | Plymouth rock or grizzle cock, with a dark red Indian game cock wound through |

been limited. He had been invalided out of the army during the Second World War, in 1943, having contracted polio while on leave, and returned from service in India on a hospital ship. Earlier, as the only officer who could not ride a motor bike, he had been put in charge of a newly formed motor cycle platoon, following the retreat from France in 1940. He learned to ride a motor bike largely thanks to the help of one Lance Corporal Harry Tout.

Although he was in a wheelchair, Deane followed the Culmstock Otter Hounds and became a very keen fisherman, having been introduced to the sport by the man who serviced his motorized wheelchair. He tied his first flies on 10 March 1948, and one of them was used soon afterwards by Ted Snow, the works manager at the garage, who caught three brace of trout with it. His regular chats about fly fishing played a major role in encouraging Deane to start tying flies and learning to fish.

An advertisement in *The Fishing Gazette* for the Exe Valley Trout Hatcheries, Dulverton, took him to Devon. The hatchery had some natural blue poultry that he wanted to see but when he arrived he found that it had closed some weeks earlier. He went into Dulverton and found the local fishing tackle shop. Looking in through the window he saw a familiar face looking back. It was his old friend Harry Tout, ex-Somerset Light Infantry Motor Cycle Platoon and son of the famous Fred Tout. Deane was introduced to Fred and told him that he had started a fly-tying business. Fred gave him three patterns, saying that if he never tied any others, he would not starve if he tied those three. One of them was, of course, the Beige.

Fred Tout made a brief appearance – 'immortalized' was the word Deane used – in Negley Farson's ever-popular book *Going Fishing* (first published in 1942). Writing about fishing the West Country of England, he described Fred Tout thus:

*Perhaps it is better to buy your casts and flies from the fishing-fanatic in the little town nearby. He stains his own casts and ties his own flies and is so covered with flies stuck into his coat and hat himself that he looks like a veritable cockleburr . . . This person, who runs the local bicycle and tackle shop, will leave his shop on the slightest excuse merely to catch a fish. He had, I believe, one or two anonymous flies with which he has experimented himself. But the ones he will probably recommend you are the small hackled blue upright – with most of the hackle snipped off; the Hare's Ears, Pheasant Tail, Greenwell's Glory, and, as the season gets on, the apparently irresistible Little Tup.*

He was still wearing the same hat when Deane met him all those years later. Incidentally, Peter Deane trimmed the bottom of the hackle of his Terry's Terrors for the first two or three years that he tied them commercially. Terry's Terror was named after Dr Cecil Terry, an eminent Bath surgeon.

When he got home to Hemyock he tied some Beiges which he wanted to use the next day on the Culm, when he was to fish with Cecil Terry, who said that they would be a good olive imitation. Like Captain Wills before him, Deane had instant success with the fly. The fly was to become so popular on the Culm that by the start of the next season he was getting orders for it for many other Devon rivers, including the Otter.

A year or two after the start of his tying business, Deane wanted to tie some Beiges to use with Ted Snow, whom he had invited to fish the Culm Flyfisher Club's waters. His usual supplier of dark red Indian game cock hackles sent him not complete capes, as was usual, but feathers that had been plucked from the cape and wrapped in newspaper. This made them difficult to sort, size and store, so he threw them away – a decision he regretted for the rest of his fly-tying days as he had thrown away 'pure gold' without realizing it. To tie the flies for his day with Ted Snow, Deane used some hackles from a packet. These feathers had over-long fibres and most had pronounced curls at the tips, as had the feathers that he threw away. The next day the two of them become aware of how well these sparsely dressed flies floated. This was appreciated by the trout too. That evening he thought about the performance of the flies and realized that he had come across what fellow fly dressers referred to as 'spring'. He then changed the size of hackles that he used for the Beige, making them slightly larger than normal for the size of hook. In his tying instructions he said that the 'hackles should be nearly twice as long in the fibres as those used on a normal size 14 dry fly'.

When he started to tie the Beige with longer hackles, he decided to change its name to the Beacon Beige. He named it after a beacon set up to warn of the impending arrival of the Spanish Armada, the Culmstock Beacon, which he could see from the window of his fly-tying room, and which was a prominent feature of the surrounding countryside. Later, he registered the name as a trade mark.

*Ranunculus is the hallmark weed of the classic English chalk stream*

He took the Beacon Beige to the River Test in 1952 when he was invited to fish a beat at Whitchurch. Although it was a filthy, windy day he fished his Beacon Beige and reached his limit in just thirty-three minutes. It did not take long for the fly to become an established pattern on the Test and also the Itchen. Deane also used it to catch sea trout and he maintained that it fished well as an adult buzzer on still waters.

A year or two later it was to be taken up and promoted by another former army officer, Dermot Wilson. He had served with distinction in the Second World War – he was awarded the Military Cross – and on his retirement from the army joined J. Walter Thompson, a notable London advertising agency, before starting the first UK Orvis shop at the mill at Nether Wallop. This he ran from 1968 to 1981.

In Dermot Wilson's first book, *Dry-Fly Beginnings* published in 1957, he advocated the use of the orange quill to represent the BWO as advised by G.E.M. Skues. This book was republished as *Fishing the Dry Fly* and in the third edition, 1987, he was promoting the Beacon Beige. On the front flap of *Dry-Fly Beginnings* Dermot Wilson, who was thirty-two when his book was published, was described as 'one of our younger "authorities" on fishing', who had fished ever since he could remember.

When it came to tying the Beacon Beige, Peter Deane was insistent that it should not be over hackled – two turns of the Plymouth rock, or grizzle, and three of the Indian game for a size 14 and half a turn less of the Indian game for a size 16. He recommended using peacock quills for the body, from the left-hand side of the eye feather, as one can tie them with the darker side of the quill uppermost and produce a nice contrasting stripe.

# ELK HAIR
# CADDIS

*Al Troth – USA*

THE ELK HAIR CADDIS was first tied by Al Troth in 1957, when he was in his mid-twenties, to represent a green sedge that trout were taking on the Loyalsock Creek, near Williamsport. His first version was tied with a cream elk hair wing, a green body and a ginger hackle. The pattern was an instant hit with the trout and he started tying it commercially in 1961.

It has the shape and colour of many different sedge or caddis flies that live in waters around the world and hatch on and off throughout much of the season. It captures the essential characteristics of many of the flies that trout eat all season long and it is for this reason that as well as being a first-class caddis imitation, it is a world-class searching pattern. Al Troth studied the fly's silhouette by placing a mirror in the bottom of a bowl of water, as it was the silhouette as seen by trout that he wanted to match. He believed that if he succeeded in doing this, then he would catch fish. As he always tried to be a practical fly tier, he felt that the fly did not need antennae or eyes or any other adornments, just the best silhouette.

Troth was a school teacher in Montgomery, Pennsylvania, who moved west to Dillon, Montana, where he was a fly tier for nearly sixty years, an outfitter and a fishing guide for almost forty years. He and his wife Martha grew up in the Pittsburgh area, but moved 250 miles north-east to the Williamsport area to

# ELK HAIR CADDIS

| | |
|---|---|
| **HOOK:** | Partridge E1A or L2A Capt Hamilton, size 6–24 |
| **THREAD:** | Tan or brown 6/0 or 8/0 |
| **RIB:** | 0.005 in. brass wire |
| **BODY:** | Hare body fur |
| **HACKLE:** | Furnace cock, palmered, with upper fibres trimmed |
| **WING:** | Natural tan or bleached cow elk or deer body hair |
| **HEAD:** | Clipped ends of elk hair wing |

teach. They lived in Muncy; Al taught in Montgomery and Martha in Hughesville, four or five miles away.

When they and their son Eric arrived in Dillon in 1973, Al started tying flies commercially for seven months of the year and guiding on the Beaverhead and Bighole Rivers. He has designed other flies although the Elk Hair Caddis is probably the best known and most widely used. He was inspired in his fly tying by the work of the famous Catskill fly tiers Harry and Elsie Darbee and Walt and Winnie Dette. G.E.M. Skues's fly, the Little Red Sedge, was an inspiration – particularly the way that Skues tied it – when Troth was developing the Elk Hair Caddis.

A former fellow guide, Paul Updike, described Troth as 'a micrometer-measuring kind of guy' who made many of his own fly-tying tools including a hackle gauge and a hair stacker, and even an underwater housing for his camera. His familiarity with a micrometer was instilled in him by his father who was a machinist in Monessen and taught his only son how to machine metal and

*A carefree trout enjoying life in this beautifully clear water*

check the results for accuracy with a micrometer. As a youngster learning to tie flies, he taught himself by dismantling commercially produced flies to see how they had been tied. During his years as a professional tier he kept all his customers' orders and fly specifications in a card index system so that he could repeat old orders precisely, even down to the number of wraps and thickness of lead wire on the hooks.

Troth tied the Elk Hair Caddis with a short, neatly trimmed head. Try to use elk hair that ties down well but, at the same time, is not so soft that it flares excessively. As well as always striving to be practical in his tying, Troth wanted to tie tough, durable flies which he did by applying rod varnish at each stage. He liked his flies to be 'proven catchers of trout, reasonably simple and quick to tie, durable, and constructed of materials that are readily available'.

The Elk Hair Caddis is a truly versatile fly that can be fished to represent different naturals depending on the size used. When fished in large sizes it can imitate a stonefly and in smaller sizes it represents both caddis and small stones. Although the pattern is probably most effective when tied in the subdued body colours that Troth favoured, it can also be tied in a range of colours including tan, olive, grey, yellow and even chartreuse.

# MONTANA

*Lew Oatman – USA*

THE ENGLISH FLY TIER Peter Deane claims to have introduced the Montana nymph to England in the mid-1950s. He was living in Devon, and was about to move to Sussex when he received a letter from Lew Oatman, a professional fly tier living in Shushan, New York State. Oatman, who died in 1958, had included a number of patterns in his letter, patterns which he specialized in tying, primarily hackled streamers and bucktails. He developed seventeen patterns, one of which was a Montana nymph tied as Lew Oatman had designed it. Deane wrote in his very good and informative book, *Peter Deane's Fly-tying*, that it 'was quite different from anything I had seen to date' and that he was 'staggered' to see that the fly had a 'pair of long slender black wings which stood out over the eye'. He then received an order from an old client in Kenya, who wanted six dozen assorted wet flies, including something different from the usual patterns. He included a dozen Montanas tied as per the example from Lew Oatman. The fly proved to be a great success in Kenya and Deane was asked to supply more – some with the thorax in different colours. This would have been the start of the many different variations in the original pattern that are so popular today.

Lew Oatman fished the Battenkill River near to the border between New York State and Vermont. In the American magazine *Fly Fisherman*, he was described as 'an early pioneer in developing feathered imitations of forage fish common to the area where he lived'. Many years ago Ted Niemeyer wrote that his 'ability to select and blend appropriate materials for the various patterns was as responsible for their success as was his talent in assembling them. He

## MONTANA

| | |
|---|---|
| **HOOK:** | Mustad 9572, size 4–14 |
| **THREAD:** | Black 3/0 or 6/0 |
| **TAIL:** | Black cock hackle fibres or black cock hackle tips, not too long |
| **BODY:** | First three-fifths black chenille |
| **THORAX:** | Yellow chenille |
| **THORAX COVER/WING CASE:** | Two strands of black chenille pulled forward over thorax |
| **HACKLE:** | Black cock, palmered through thorax only |
| **WINGS:** | Long, slender black rook or crow primary, tied forward over the hook eye |

belongs in the company of tiers such as Carrie Stevens, Jim Leisenring and Jack Atherton.' He went on: 'To understand Lew's tying objectives, you must understand that he copied specific baitfish.' In this he sought exact imitation, which tends to suggest that his Montana nymph was outside his normal parameters. The typical Oatman fly had a cigar-shaped body, which is in contrast to the somewhat chunky body of the Montana nymph.

After this episode, the fly disappeared, according to Deane, until it reappeared in about 1987 when it was referred to in angling reports in the British magazine *Trout and Salmon*. But no reference to the pattern mentioned the original wings. He suggested that anglers who had fished the unwinged version with success might like to see what happened with an original winged version.

The dressing given here is that claimed by Peter Deane to be the original. Modern dressings are identical apart from the absence of the wings.

## PHEASANT TAIL NYMPH

| | |
|---|---|
| **HOOK:** | Down eye Limerick, size 16–20 |
| **WEIGHT/THREAD:** | Fine red-colour copper wire |
| **TAILS:** | Tips of four fibres from a browny-red cock pheasant centre tail feather |
| **BODY:** | As tails |
| **THORAX:** | As tails |

# PHEASANT TAIL NYMPH

*Frank Sawyer – England*

FRANK SAWYER WAS THE river keeper for the Services Dry-fly Fishing Association's 6½ miles of the Wiltshire Avon. He was born in 1906 in a cottage in Bulford and became keeper in 1928, at just twenty-two, when it was the Officers' Fishing Association waters (the name was changed in 1964). In the same year he saw his first fish caught on a nymph fished by Brigadier General H.E. Carey, the honorary secretary. Before starting work as a keeper on his own, he had been under-keeper to Frederick Martin, who was Colonel Bailey's head keeper. Most of Sawyer's nymph fishing in his early years was for grayling, which provided him with very good schooling for when he went on to fish for trout. Sawyer published his first book, *Keeper of the Stream*, in 1952, based on twenty-four years of experience of looking after and maintaining a chalk stream trout fishery. He died on 18 April 1980, on the bank of his beloved Avon when he was taking his dog for a walk. A plain wooden seat was erected to mark the spot.

Frank Sawyer will always be associated with his Pheasant Tail Nymph. This simple fly must be one of the most widely fished – and most successful – artificial flies of all time. It has caught fish in virtually every country where anglers fly fish for trout. Although it is one of the simplest of patterns, tied from just two materials – fibres from a cock pheasant tail feather (the older the better) and very fine, red dish copper wire – it has not been bettered as a representative of olive nymphs when tied in different sizes. Although designed originally for use on rivers, it has proved to be equally effective on still waters. Fly tiers have sought to tie many variations, some of which have lost the elegance of the original, but as conceived by Frank Sawyer it still proves to be the best.

The inspiration for the fly came from Sawyer's favourite dry fly, the Pheasant Tail Red Spinner. In 1965 he wrote: 'This nymph was actually a follow-up of my Pheasant Tail Red Spinner which I found would take fish after it had lost all its hackles and sank.'

Although he had the basis for a nymph pattern, it was to be quite some time before he developed a method of tying it that incorporated some weight so that it would sink quickly but without unnecessary bulk and without affecting the neatness of the artificial. Too bulky a pattern would look unattractive as well as not penetrating the water quickly enough. The breakthrough came when he discovered that he could use fine wire both to weight (or ballast, to use his word), the fly and to construct it. Sawyer claimed to have been the first to tie nymphs using only copper wire for 'base building, ballasting, and the tying in of the pheasant tail fibres'. He chose wires that were 'of a colouring to suit and tone in with the general dressing'. Although tying flies with wire only can be difficult at first, once one is used to it, it works very well. It is therefore somewhat surprising that no other patterns are tied in this way, particularly now that there is such an enormous range of suitable wires in many different colours and shades.

One difficulty to be overcome by anyone lacking experience in tying flies with wire only is anchoring the wire to the hook firmly enough to stop it revolving round the shank of the hook while tying the fly as well as holding the finished body in place. It is very easy to break fine wire – Sawyer described the wire that he used as a little thicker than a human hair – by trying to wrap it round the hook too firmly. It can help to anchor the wire to the hook by tying it on in the conventional way (as with thread) for two or three turns, taking a couple more turns round the hook shank on the other side of the tag end and then making more turns on the hook eye side, building up the thorax in the process. When this has been done, trim off the tag end and take the wire in touching turns to the hook bend, to where you want to tie-in the

*The River Avon in Wiltshire where Frank Sawyer developed the Pheasant Tail Nymph*

pheasant tail fibres which make up the tails and the body. Sawyer actually took the wire to the hook bend and then forward to make the thorax and back again, so covering the hook with three layers of wire.

When he had tied-in the tails, which should be only an eighth of an inch long, he wrapped the pheasant tail fibres round the wire for reinforcing, and then wrapped the fibres and the wire in touching turns to the hook eye, where he separated them. He then took the wire back behind the thorax and bent the

*Original Pheasant Tail Nymphs tied by Frank Sawyer*

fibres back over the thorax and fastened them with a turn of wire before taking the wire forward again. He then made a second, forward lap of fibres, secured them with a turn of wire and took the wire back to the end of the thorax. He finished it with a third wrap of the pheasant fibres over the thorax which he secured behind the thorax with a couple of half hitches. He took the wire forward and secured it, with a whip finish or some half hitches, behind the eye of the hook. Finally, he trimmed the ends of the fibres neatly. All genuine Sawyer Pheasant Tail Nymphs were tied with the fibres tied and trimmed off at the back of the thorax and not behind the eye.

For Sawyer, 'Nymph fishing, when carried out as it should be, is, I think, the most fascinating of all kinds of angling.' And in the heat of summer when the light and low and clear water provided the best conditions for seeing fish in their feeding positions, it was 'the most difficult angling art'. Through his work as a river keeper he brought a completely new approach to nymph fishing, based on his observation of the habits and movements of nymphs in the water and the way that trout and grayling fed on them.

He liked to use a fly that appeared to be 'translucent and gives the effect of air beneath the nymphal shuck'. Nymphs must be cast with the accuracy and delicacy of a dry fly. He designed and tied his nymphs so that they had a quick entry into the water and would then sink rapidly to the required depth. General shape and colour, together with size, were the key points that Sawyer wanted to represent, rather than exact imitation.

*I am in favour of exact representation for dry-fly or nymph, but when I use the word representation I try to carry it into effect. I want representation that is satisfactory from the trout's point of view. A correct imitation of the colouring and shape of an insect is not enough. To represent truly an insect, and successfully deceive a trout, the artificial must be offered at a time when he is taking, or likely to be taking, the natural from or beneath the surface of the water; offered in such a manner that it looks alive, or dead, or in a semi-inert stage, as natural ones are at the moment.*

# PRINCE NYMPH

| | |
|---|---|
| **HOOK:** | Standard nymph, 2X long, Mustad 9671 down eye 2XL, size 8–20 |
| **THREAD:** | Black 6/0 or 8/0, according to size |
| **WEIGHT:** | Lead wire, optional |
| **TAILS:** | Brown turkey or goose biots |
| **RIB:** | Oval gold tinsel |
| **BODY:** | Peacock herl |
| **HACKLE:** | Brown or furnace hen |
| **WINGS OR HORNS:** | White turkey or goose biots, tied in a wide 'V' on top of the body, flared upwards |

# PRINCE NYMPH

*Doug Prince – USA*

IS THIS A GENERIC attractor nymph or a pattern that has a hatch to match? Given enough time spent searching for naturals and a creative imagination, it is possible to match many a weird-and-wonderful artificial with a natural. Could the Prince nymph be so effective because it is a 'blend of the familiar and the unusual – a familiar mayfly shape with unusual horns to attract the trout's curiosity'?

It seems to have started life as the Brown Forked Tail nymph around 1950. This name is easy to understand when you see the pattern, with its forked biots. Or should this be the Black Forked Tail nymph, as some authorities suggest that the Brown Forked Tail nymph is a variation of the Prince nymph? However, it is now generally accepted that this fly carries Doug Prince's name. He lived in Monterey, California, and fished the King's River. One account credits Don and Dick Olson of Bemidji, Minnesota, with its invention, saying it was then named after Prince, who promoted it and made it popular.

It would seem to have been in anglers' fly boxes for at least forty years and is likely to continue to be there for many years to come.

## ZUG BUG

| | |
|---|---|
| HOOK: | Mustad 3906B or 9671, size 10 2X long – 14 2X long |
| WEIGHT: | Lead wire as required |
| THREAD: | Black 6/0 |
| TAIL: | Three to six peacock sword fibres, tied short |
| RIB: | Fine oval silver, three turns only |
| BODY: | Peacock herl |
| HACKLE: | Brown hen neck, tied as a wet fly collar hackle, one turn only |
| WING PAD: | Mallard flank feather or wood duck flank feather, clipped short |

# ZUG BUG

*J. Clifford Zug – USA*

CLIFF ZUG'S NYMPH WAS designed to have a wide application and so it has. It is known as Old Faithful on the Firehole River because of its unfailing effectiveness, owing largely to the subtle coloration and iridescence of the peacock herls used for its body and tail. Charles Brooks was uncertain whether it is a suggestive or impressionistic pattern but he was certain that it is a very effective general nymph pattern when fished in waters where there are dark-bodied naturals.

Information on Zug himself is hard to come by. He was an outdoor writer for the *Reading Pennsylvania Record* in the 1950s. At this time, the magazine *Field and Stream* used to have a short article in each issue written by A.J. McClane. In one of his articles, he wrote about a visit Zug made to the Old Brick Red Mill Trout Club, in 1955, when he had 'a banner day' resulting in seven brown trout weighing from 2 lb to 5 lb. Later Zug fished at Fisherman's Paradise at Bellefont, Pennsylvania, where he caught a 6³/₄ lb brown. He also used the fly that we know as the Zug Bug on the Allagash in Maine, where it was very effective for catching numerous brook trout, and later in Ontario, Canada. In Wayne Buszek's *Buz's Catalogue* for 1965, there are three sentences on the Zug Bug: 'The Kemp's Bug went east and J. Cliff Zug came up with this version. Equally successful I prefer it personally and unless you insist on the Kemp Bug I will send this pattern. Imitates a great many underwater forms of food.'

Randall Kaufman included the dressing for the Kemp's Bug in his book *American Nymph Fly Tying Manual*. It is basically the same as the Zug Bug but it has grizzly hackle tip wings tied short. Many believe it is more effective but it does not seem to have been mentioned for years.

Anssi Uitti, a Finnish outdoor writer and fly fisherman, is a great fan of the Zug Bug. He fishes mainly for brown trout in southern and central Finland, with old cane rods that he has collected and restored himself – according to his wife he has too many! The Zug Bug has been his favourite searching nymph for the last fifteen years or so.

As he says, it is not an imitative pattern, but like so many effective general nymphs it bears a resemblance to many kinds of trout food such as cased caddis and stonefly and damselfly nymphs. He has always had a deep attachment to wet flies and nymphs with peacock bodies. There is something magical in the green

*A bridge over a river is as attractive to fish as to anglers*

sheen of the peacock herl which seems to attract fish as much as fishermen. He used to use the Lead-winged Coachman nymph as a searching pattern, but switched to the Zug Bug because it has more flash, thanks to the distinctive oval silver rib and lighter wing pad – a definite advantage in a universal searching nymph. Both patterns sport the single triangular-shaped wing pad, which gives them a very 'stoneflyish' silhouette.

The Zug Bug is fished best in the traditional style: upstream on a longish leader with or without a strike indicator. Even though the fly may seem an unlikely choice for educated trout, Uitti has caught many good wild brown trout from heavily fished waters on it, both in the smaller rivers and brooks of southern Finland and in the bigger, turbulent rivers of the central area. Tie some Zug Bugs with plenty of weight for fishing similar big, brawling rivers. Uitti has also found it to be a solid choice for rainbows in rivers and brook trout in small spring-fed brooks. It is also a reliable pattern for grayling, especially in the late autumn and winter.

Peacock herl is not one of the toughest or most durable materials, but one tip I came across for improving the durability of a fly with a peacock herl body is to wrap the herl or herls around your tying thread, making them into a rope and then wrapping the rope round the hook shank in the normal way. The herls will now be reinforced by the tying thread. One other point to note is that on the Zug Bug the wing case or pad is tied-in differently from many other patterns in that it lies flat over the body but is tied-in only at the front, just behind the eye of the hook. It is not tied down at the rear. Some recipes suggest that the mallard flank feather should be dyed to match the colour of a wood duck feather.

*Flymph Original*

## FLYMPH

| | |
|---|---|
| **HOOK:** | Partridge Flashpoint TWH The Wet, size 8–18 |
| **THREAD:** | Dark brown UNI-thread 8/0 |
| **RIB:** | Fine gold wire |
| **BODY:** | Cream and dark brown hare's fur |
| **HACKLE:** | Grey partridge |

# FLYMPH

*James E. Leisenring and Vernon S. 'Pete' Hidy – USA*

THE FLYMPH IS A cross between a nymph and a (dry) fly and it represents very well the stage of emergence of a hatching nymph or caddis pupa. It is a soft-hackle nymph that is fished to represent hatching mayflies and caddis. James E. Leisenring and Vernon S. 'Pete' Hidy co-authored *The Art of Tying the Wet Fly and Fishing the Flymph*, which was published originally under Leisenring's name as *The Art of Tying the Wet Fly* in 1941. And it was Hidy who coined the name flymph in 1963.

Leisenring, who was from Pennsylvania, spent thirty years between 1910 and 1940 experimenting and testing different techniques and flies on a range of trout streams in the eastern and western states of the USA. His favourite way of catching trout was with his soft-hackle nymphs, which he used to simulate hatching mayflies and caddis. It was the technique that he developed for fishing these patterns that made him famous and became known as the Leisenring Lift. Throughout his life he sought to stay 'in tune with the river'.

Hidy wrote: 'Leisenring developed and perfected his lift technique by trying to please trout swirling and feeding just beneath the surface or, quite often, by teasing and coaxing trout to feed during a lull.' When he spotted a trout swirling in the water, he would position himself so that he could cast upstream and a little way beyond the fish. The cast would be followed by a tug on the line to straighten the leader. This would ensure that he was in direct contact with his fly. As it approached the fish, he raised the rip of his rod from near the water as high as necessary, depending on the depth and speed of the river. This action

*Flymph Danica*

would make the soft hackles and the natural fur of the body quiver and move, at the same time lifting the fly in the water, as though it was rising to the surface to hatch out and escape. He used this method to fish only for fish that he could see or when casting to a known lie.

Hidy's account of the Leisenring Lift is a development of how Leisenring himself described the way he fished his flies. He tied his flies 'to act lifelike and look lifelike' and fished them to appear lifelike and 'become deadly at the point where the trout is most likely to take his food'. He did not try to impart any fancy movements to his fly with his rod but at all times kept his line taut without actually pulling on the fly so that it moved unnaturally. When his fly had reached the area of the feeding fish, he stopped following it with his rod tip. When he checked his rod, the fly would be lifted in the water by the pressure of

*Hidy Flymph*

the current on the line and leader. As his fly rose in the water, its hackles would open and close to give the effect of a living and breathing insect. As he wrote: 'The water will do all that is necessary to make a fly deadly if it is properly tied.'

Charles E. Brooks wrote that he was convinced that it was the technique that caught fish, regardless of the pattern of fly used, although he had more confidence of success if his artificial 'had some resemblance to the natural'. And the Leisenring Lift would catch fish on the most outrageous patterns, if carried out correctly. He regarded it 'as the deadliest of all nymph techniques, properly used, for taking larger trout'.

Leisenring was careful to select materials that would make his flies both act and look alive. He developed the dubbing brush for making the bodies of his flymphs, using the Clark spinning block. He was insistent that natural furs must be used, never anything artificial. Natural furs, including muskrat, mole, Arctic fox, grey or red fox and hare have better textures and more subtle, natural colours. The best is hair from the face, cheeks, poll and ears of an English hare's mask. Natural fur is water resistant and will trap small bubbles of air. He spun his bodies using waxed thread (most likely Pearsall's silks) in subtle colours to enhance the natural fur, including ash, olive-yellow and crimson – with mole fur – and made them in batches which he stored on a piece of card with notches on both sides. 'Desirable hackles are those from the necks of partridge and starling.' He tied small wet flies with 'a careful attention to action-giving qualities, size, form and color'.

'Pete' Hidy recommended using Mustad 94842 TUE, a good light-wire hook, or a wide-gape up-eye hook with a short shank for caddis flies, in sizes 12–16. Mayfly flymphs should be tied on standard length hooks in sizes 10–18.

*Swedish Lapland, a paradise for those anglers who seek and appreciate solitude*

# RACKELHANEN

*Kenneth Boström – Sweden*

THE CADDIS (TRICHOPTERA) IS a very prolific fly and there are a great many different varieties, with some 260 species in Sweden alone. Caddis, or sedge, flies have been ignored in many countries where their importance as a source of food for trout was often unrecognized. Unlike mayflies (*Ephemeroptera*), caddis pass through four stages in their development: egg, larva, pupa and finally adult. It is the larvae of most species that live in cases made from whatever materials are available, including tiny pieces of stick, grains of sand and even tiny shells. Those living in running water use heavy materials so that they are not swept away by the current. The adults are found in a range of colours and sizes and it can be difficult to identify them correctly. As the cased caddis are the most abundant, they are of greatest interest to the trout fisherman. An understanding of how they behave when hatching and laying eggs is helpful.

The Swedish fly Rackelhanen is a caddis pattern that was developed in 1967 by Kenneth Boström during a caddis hatch on the Vännån which flows between the counties of Kronoberg and Halland in southern Sweden. The fish were being very selective, feeding on a caddis pupa that hatched just below the surface at a depth of about 10–20 cm. Although the pupae were easy prey anywhere from the river bed to the surface, the fish were interested in feeding on them only in a very restricted zone and were not interested in the hatched flies on the surface before they flew off. Fortunately for Boström the hatch continued for a number of evenings, which gave him time to experiment and eventually develop a successful artificial, the Rackelhanen.

## RACKELHANEN

HOOK: Light wire, down eye, size 10–18
THREAD: Same colour as body and wing
BODY: Dubbed with chopped-up polypropylene yarn either brown,
beige, olive, grey or black
WING: Polypropylene yarn, same colour as body
THORAX: Polypropylene yarn, same colour as body

It took him some time to work out just what was happening but when he understood the problem of these hatching pupae and how to imitate them, he had to find the correct material, tying method and then the fishing technique. The material was to be polypropylene yarn of a colour that is the best match for your local caddis. One point that Boström stresses is that the fly must always be treated with a good floatant (originally he recommended Permafloat) because many anglers do not understand that polypropylene does not float by itself: it must be treated to make it do so.

Once he had produced the finished design, Boström was reluctant to show it to his fishing friends because it did not look attractive. In fact one said that it looked like a 'bastard'. The Rackelhanen is named after the extremely rare offspring of a capercaillie (*tjäder* in Swedish) and a black grouse (*orre*). But initial laughter at its appearance and scepticism about its efficiency changed quickly to admiration when friends found out just how effective it was when fished correctly. The attraction of the pattern to trout and also char, rainbow, cutthroat trout and grayling, is down to the fact that it has a fuzzy and indistinct silhouette when looked at against the sky from underneath. A caddis is never still on or in the water, they are always skittering and buzzing about and look indistinct and fuzzy.

Boström was born in 1945 and started fly fishing as a boy in Småland in southern Sweden. From his earliest days with a fly rod in his hand, he was interested in the mayflies and sedges that trout feed on. He then became very worried about the effect of acid rain on the insects and fly-life of his Småland streams and initiated a number of river conservation projects in the late 1960s. In the 1980s he published a booklet on rivers and streams, *Mayflies in Trout Waters*, and later *Sedges in Trout Waters*, which made it easier for Scandinavian fly fishers to identify and imitate what is hatching when they are on the river. He also developed a composite bamboo/carbon-fibre fly rod with what is described as an 'exquisite parabolic action'. After forty years of rod building he is still making about ten Rackelhanen rods each year.

Since 1967 Boström has developed a number of different ways to fish the fly, usually in the surface film on a floating line, but sometimes a sink-tip can be a better choice. Exactly how you fish the pattern depends on what the particular caddis you are trying to imitate are doing. For example, stripping the fly back in very short, jerky, nervous pulls with a brief pause between, imitates egg-laying

*Ready to be released*

or drinking caddis. When he sees fish taking caddis pupae that are swimming or paddling on the surface of a river, he trims the wing and then presents the fly as a pupa heading for the bank or land. Fished floating free – as a normal dry fly – the Rackelhanen can imitate a spent caddis. Another technique, which can be successful with a short sink-tip, is to let the leader sink so that the fly is pulled under water. Pause and then let the fly float up again in imitation of a caddis hatching just below the surface.

When tying the fly, choose waxed tying thread and polypropylene yarn of a colour that best matches your local caddis, mixing two or more colours if necessary. To make the dubbing for the body, cut the yarn into short pieces about 10 mm long and fluff up. Wind the first two turns of the dubbed thread down towards the bend and then back to the front of the hook, leaving plenty of space for the wings and front body or thorax. Doing this helps trap the fibres of the first turns in the right position. Cut a length of yarn for the wings and tie down in the middle. Fold the yarn back and tie down over the base of the wing, so that the two lengths of yarn are side by side. The wings should not be too long and should be trimmed so that they extend to the bend of the hook. Dub the thread again with chopped lengths of yarn and make the thorax. Finish the fly by tying a neat head.

Boström does not use any particular make or type of hook for the Rackel-hanen. Even when tied on wet fly hooks, the fly will ride high when treated properly with floatant.

# RED FOX SQUIRREL-HAIR NYMPH

| | |
|---|---|
| **HOOK:** | Tiemco 5262 (standard and bead head); Tiemco 2313, 2302 (caddis emerger) and Tiemco 2457 (scud), size 2–20 |
| **THREAD:** | Black or orange 6/0 Danville waxed Flymaster |
| **WEIGHT:** | Lead wire, diameter of hook wire, 8 to 12 turns |
| **TAIL:** | Small tuft of back fur from red fox squirrel skin |
| **RIB:** | Oval gold tinsel |
| **ABDOMEN:** | Belly fur from red fox squirrel skin, mixed 50/50 with sienna or fox tan Antron dubbing or Dave Whitlock SLF dubbing No. 1 |
| **THORAX:** | Back fur from red fox squirrel skin, mixed 50/50 with charcoal Antron dubbing or Dave Whitlock SLF Dubbing No. 2 |
| **LEGS:** | On sizes 10 and larger tan and brown chicken hen neck or back hackle or partridge, one turn |
| **CEMENT:** | Dave Whitlock's Flexament and Zap-A-Gap |

# RED FOX SQUIRREL-HAIR NYMPH

*Dave Whitlock – USA*

IF MOST ANGLERS WERE restricted – horror of horrors – to just one pattern of artificial fly, it would have to be a pattern like the classic Gold-Ribbed Hare's Ear, Adams dry fly or Woolly Bugger streamer, that performs well for most fly fishers in most waters. If Dave Whitlock were to be restricted to one, he would choose his Red Fox Squirrel-Hair nymph. It is the most consistently effective fly, both in numbers of fish caught and size that he uses. And perhaps of even greater significance, it seems to perform well almost everywhere and for whoever fishes it.

When he first began tying soft, fur-bodied nymphs in the 1960s, he was most influenced by the flies tied and fished by Thom Green, Ted Trueblood and Polly Rosborough. But he did not have the furs that they often recommended, such as otter, mink, seal, hare's ear and beaver. He substituted grey and red fox squirrels, muskrat and rabbit, which he could obtain locally for his nymphs, but was not confident that they would have the seemingly magical qualities of the three masters' nymphs. However, the Red Fox Squirrel-Hair was immediately effective and his confidence increased. Although as the years have passed he has built a fine inventory of furs, synthetic dubbing and other useful fly-tying materials, he has yet to tie a nymph pattern with any other fur that is more effective for him for all-round fly fishing.

The RFSH is an impressionistic fly. This means that it looks alive, vulnerable and edible without looking exactly like a specific creature. A trout, whether feeding actively or not, seldom ignores such a morsel swimming or drifting towards it. By maintaining the material pattern while varying its size and profile, you can make the nymph mimic numerous trout foods: certain species of mayflies, stoneflies, caddis flies, midges, damselflies, scuds, sowbugs and crayfish. It is a tempting tit-bit regardless of what a particular fish is preparing to dine on. If presented and fished like a specific live food, say an emerging caddis pupa or a swimming scud, it becomes more actively imitative rather than passively suggestive.

The material used is most responsible for the fly's effectiveness. It is tied with rich orange-tan red fox squirrel belly fur and the spicy spectrum of tan, cream, grey, black and white from the red fox squirrel back. Whitlock blends each fur with a matching glossy synthetic fibre and ribs the fly with gold oval tinsel or pearlescent gold Flashabou. This combination gives the pattern the light, natural cast so common in natural aquatic insects and crustaceans, especially during the vulnerable soft-shell stage which trout seem to prefer. The soft texture of the fur further enhances this natural image and attractiveness to fish. Water, air bubbles and light on the fur and tinsel body create additional haloes of visual liveliness and movement. The wear and natural odour absorption of extended use increases the nymph's effectiveness.

For dubbing, shave the fur directly off the hide with electric hair clippers. Cut some of the back hide into convenient $1/2$-inch wide strips for tailing material. The bridle-barred back hair of the grey or red fox squirrel also makes a marvellous addition for blending with natural hair or synthetic fibres of one plain colour. Blending gives the dubbing more character and a more natural, lifelike look. Squirrel fur also takes most dyes quickly, so tinting it olive, yellow, gold and brown makes it even more versatile. Young squirrels have finer, softer fur for dubbing smaller nymphs. Hair from summer-hunted squirrels is too thin, short and wiry for ideal dubbing. Late autumn and winter hides have the longest hair and are densely furred with the best dubbing. If you find squirrel hair that seems too short or grainy for easy dubbing, simply blend it with a small amount of longer rabbit or muskrat fur or soft, synthetic fibres.

Squirrel tail hair is completely unsatisfactory for this nymph's body or tail. Hair from the animal's body must be used. If red fox squirrel is not available, lightly dye grey fox squirrel with a tangerine or orange dye. You can substitute hare's mask for back fur and bleached muskrat, beaver or Australian opossum for belly fur. (When bleached, a medium grey fur first changes to a colour similar to the red fox squirrel's belly.)

For the standard RFSH nymph, use a 2XL hook. Weight the shank with lead wire of the same diameter as the hook wire, wrapped over the middle half of the hook shank. For natural shapes other than those that can be tied on 2XL hooks, use longer or shorter shanks. Smaller long-shank hooks also have the advantage of hooking with less strike pressure, and they seldom hang up when bounced over the bottom.

The tail is a small tuft of three or four guard hairs and underfur, equal in length to half the shank's length. It actually represents both the body extension past the bend of the hook and the tail appendages. Leave only the tan base exposed (tie down the grey base hair found next to the skin). This will give the same colour extension to the abdomen and tail base.

The abdomen should be half or two-thirds of the hook shank length, tapering to a thicker diameter forward over the lead wraps. On very small hooks, sizes 14–18, clip off the long free ends of the guard hairs on the abdomen to help the nymph sink. For hook sizes 16 and smaller, use the finest, shortest squirrel hair.

For the rib on the smaller sizes (16 to 20), use gold wire. For size 14 to 10 hooks use the smallest size oval tinsel (size 18) and from 8 to 2, use size 16 or 14 oval tinsel. The rib does not necessarily suggest body segmentation when wrapped over the dubbing. It gives a definite illusion of transparency and lifelike movement in the water.

The thorax should be enlarged compared to the abdomen and should be loosely wound so that guard-hair tips will radiate off this section to simulate legs, wing cases, antennae and gills. If you want to simulate the larger leggy stoneflies, damsel nymphs and caddis pupae, you can make one turn of a soft webby cree, dark grizzly or brown partridge feather immediately in front of the thorax and trim off all but six or eight of the fibres.

Minor variations in body colours seem to make little difference to the effectiveness of this fly. At times Whitlock even mixes additional bits of olive, fluorescent orange, fluorescent green or red and black into the dubbing for a wider colour choice to cope with water colour, clarity, natural colours and other variations.

To fish the RFSH nymph vary your presentation to suit the water type and depth and natural action of the nymph that the fish would be most likely to key on. The most consistent way to catch trout on the RFSH in streams is to fish it dead drift, just off the bottom, using a long knotless tapered leader and a floating line.

# SOUTH PLATTE BRASSIE

*Gene Lynch, Ken Chandler and Tug Davenport – USA*

THE SOUTH PLATTE BRASSIE, a midge larva imitation, is a minimalist pattern similar to the late Oliver Kite's Bare Hook nymph which was a hook with a thorax only made from copper wire. It was described once as a 'pheasant-less Pheasant Tail nymph'. Although fishing midge larva imitations has been associated more closely with still waters than rivers, more anglers are now aware of the frequency with which trout feed on midges in running water.

Three Colorado anglers and fly tiers, Gene Lynch, Ken Chandler and Tug Davenport, are credited with creating this pattern in the 1960s. Did it come about as the result of an accident, or was it an intentional design? Local research has failed to produce a definitive answer. The pattern is named after the South Platte River in Colorado although it is known popularly as just the Brassie. The wire used to tie it simulates the segmentation of the abdomen of a midge or caddis larva or pupa, as well as providing the weight necessary to get the fly down to the fish.

One of the problems with this pattern in its early years was that the fine gauge plain copper wire became tarnished very easily. This problem was so bad that commercially tied flies were sold in individual gelatin capsules to stop the wire from oxidizing. Forty years and more later, original examples in their capsules still look as good as new. This problem has been eliminated with the use of modern coated copper wires.

*Brassie with peacock herl thorax*

## SOUTH PLATTE BRASSIE

HOOK: Tiemco 200R sizes 16–22, Mustad 9671 or 94840, size 8–24 and smaller

THREAD: Black, 8/0 or finer

BODY: Copper wire, size to suit hook

THORAX: Fine black dubbing or two turns of peacock or ostrich herl

The original South Platte Brassie had a thorax made from black heat-shrink tubing, but this has been replaced in current tyings by either fine black dubbing or a couple of turns of peacock or ostrich herl. Another development is to tie the pattern with a two-colour body, using two different wires, for example black and copper, red and silver or green and copper. For those who want to stick closely to the original pattern, suitable diameters of wire are now available in a wide range of shades of copper as well as other suitable colours.

Although this is a simple pattern, requiring but two materials, it can present something of a challenge in tying the copper wire in close, tight touching turns. The easiest way to tie this pattern is to wrap the copper wire around the bare shank of the hook, as this makes it easier to wrap the wire in turns that actually touch the preceding one. To lock the wire in place, pinch each end tight against the hook shank. You can add a spot of superglue to the end of the wire by the bend of the hook. The tying thread used to secure the peacock or ostrich herl or black dubbing can be used to lock the end of the wire behind the eye of the hook.

*Brassie with a heat-shrink tube thorax*

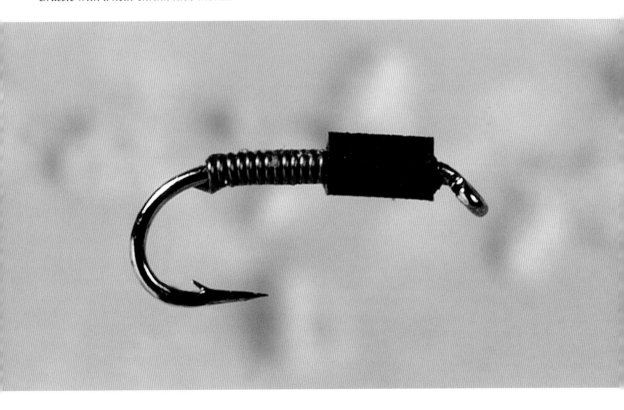

# WOOLLY BUGGER

| | |
|---|---|
| HOOK: | Mustad 79580, size 6 3X–18 2X long shank |
| THREAD: | Black 6/0 or 8/0, according to hook size |
| TAIL: | Black marabou |
| BODY: | Dark olive chenille |
| HACKLE: | Black hen or soft, webby black cock saddle hackle, palmered |

# WOOLLY BUGGER

*Russell Blessing – USA*

In Cathy Beck's book *Cathy Beck's Fly-Fishing Handbook*, there is a chapter with the wonderful title 'Woolly Buggers Don't Hatch'. While the Woolly Bugger is not the only fly to which this description might apply, streamers such as this do, in general, imitate a number of different types of small fish and other swimming invertebrates such as leeches and worms which do not hatch in the same way as mayflies, for example. So while a Woolly Bugger may not hatch, it represents a wide range of food forms enjoyed by trout. It is perhaps unsurprising that Beck used this title as it was her husband, Barry, who was responsible for first publicizing the Woolly Bugger in an article in *Fly Fisherman* magazine in May 1984.

In developing the Woolly Bugger, Russell C. Blessing, of Pennsylvania, set out to tie a better Dobson fly larva in 1967. His first attempts, with a trimmed hackle and no tail, were reported to have fished quite well but he wanted more movement in his fly, so he tried a black marabou tail and a webby black hackle, tied in by the tip and then palmered forward. He left the hackle long and untrimmed after he had seen how well it undulated when blown on. The other key ingredient was the chenille body. After Beck's article was published, Blessing became aware of the pattern's wide appeal for catching not only trout but a wide range of other fish too.

Blessing was born in Harrisburg, Pennsylvania, in 1935, and although he started fly fishing in 1956, he did not fish seriously until 1962. He started fly tying during the winter of 1962–3 when he began to develop a hellgrammite – the larva of a Dobson fly – imitation. He was very aware of the effectiveness of the hellgrammite for catching smallmouth and rock bass so it was not surprising that an imitation was one of the first flies he tried to tie. His daughter Julie named the fly that he produced eventually in 1967 when she was seven years old. She was watching him tying flies and asked, 'What's that thing?' The same question was to be asked by many others, including Barry Beck. Blessing told her: 'Well, it's sort of a Woolly Worm with a long tail. I guess a man named Woolly, an Englishman probably, tied a fly with a feather wound round the body. I put a soft, bushy tail on it.' 'Woolly Bugger!' she exclaimed. The name stuck.

For his first attempts he tied a fly with a variegated chenille or muskrat fur body with a black palmered hackle that he trimmed to a stubble. The head was built up from chenille, covered with tying thread and then lacquered well. He also tied some smaller versions in olive and green to imitate caddis larvae and similar insects. He then read an article about the Blossom fly, a salt-water pattern developed by Mark Sosin, which had a chenille body and a marabou tail. It was to play a very important part in the development of his Woolly Bugger. He tied Blossom flies with hackles and added a marabou tail to a Woolly Worm all the time trying to create a more lively hellgrammite. An untrimmed hackle resulted in more life so he stopped trimming them. His choice of colour for the body was dark olive.

He does not add weight. He has in the past used lead wire and bead heads but no longer. He prefers to carry a selection of bead heads in different materials, and add one to the tippet before tying on the fly. If you do not want to carry a selection of bead heads, a split shot can be pinched on the tippet instead. Adding weight to the tippet makes an individual fly much more versatile than if it is tied with weight. When retrieved with a slow, steady retrieve, at the same time as raising and lowering the rod tip, the fly will rise and fall in the water, with the bushy tail pulsating seductively. Cast up and across and make an upstream mend to allow the fly to sink to the required level before starting the retrieve.

Although streamers are usually tied on large hooks – typically 4s and 6s –

Blessing fishes his Woolly Buggers tied on size 12 or 16 hooks and sometimes as small as 18 2X long. When tying the pattern it is vital to make the tail the right length. It should be tied full and as long as the hook shank. Start by attaching the tying thread to the rear of the hook and then tying-in a good bunch of marabou, making sure that its length is correct. Then tie-in the tip of a suitable black saddle hackle, at the rear of the hook, and then the dark olive chenille for the body. Wind the thread forward to the hook eye and then the chenille. Tie-off the chenille at the eye. Now palmer the hackle forwards in open turns to the hook eye. Tie-off the hackle, trim the butt and whip finish the head of the fly. Complete it with a drop of varnish or head cement.

The Woolly Bugger is a versatile pattern that can be fished in different ways – upstream dead drift, across and down, and downstream – to represent different types of trout food. If the end of the marabou tail is pinched or nipped off short, it will make a passable damsel nymph imitation. And it has made a far greater impact than anyone could have imagined at the time. For Blessing the original black hackle and dark olive body version is still his favourite. He is philosophical about the many variations that are produced by other tiers, such as bead heads, ribs and the addition of a few strands of Krystal Flash to the tail. 'Fly tiers are creative by nature, so slightly changing a pattern or incorporating new ideas into an existing pattern is common practice.' And as he added, many of today's patterns can trace their ancestry back to earlier ones including, in this case, the Woolly Worm and Blossom fly.

# BUNNY

| | |
|---|---|
| **HOOK:** | Wet fly, size 4–8 |
| **THREAD:** | 6/0 red |
| **EYES:** | Bead chain. Optional |
| **BUTT:** | Red tying thread |
| **TAIL AND BODY:** | Strip of rabbit, mink, wolf, polar bear or similar hair |

# BUNNY

*Mel Krieger – USA*

MEL KRIEGER CREATED HIS Bunny fly in about 1970. Its development was inspired by a local fly, the Rabbit, which he saw in New Zealand. This fly has a long Antipodean history. The original New Zealand pattern was a Matuka-style fly with a strip of rabbit fur replacing the usual feathers. This fly also preceded Dan Byford's Zonker. Zonkers and Matukas are very effective for luring big trout, used to feeding on bait fish, from the bottom of deep pools.

Also in the 1950s Max Christensen, the expatriate Dane who became a great Tasmanian tier, used to tie countless variations of what he called a Yeti. In essence this was a small, tadpole-sized version of the Rabbit. We do not known if he got the idea from New Zealand – he certainly had not fished there – and Veniard's little booklet of Australian, New Zealand and South African flies (including the Rabbit) had not yet been published. In the book *The Fly*, Dick Wigram described the Yeti as follows:

*For this he uses a small strip of soft black fur, left on the skin and tied along the back of the hook shank. This strip is ribbed to the body of the fly with gold wire. An extremely useful fly, durable and attractive.*

The pattern had orange cock hackle fibres for the tail, a single strand of black marabou silk body and a black hackle.

Tony Sloane's Rabbit Fur fly, which has become a standard in Australia in its own right since the 1970s, is another ancestor of the Bunny. It should not be confused with other Rabbit flies from New Zealand and the USA, which are Matuka-style patterns. The trick to tying Tony Sloane's fly is in the way that the strip of rabbit skin is cut and folded. A good thick winter pelt is recommended, using the darker, long-staple fur from the lower back, and cutting a strip across the pelt, about three eighths of an inch wide and five eighths of an inch long. The strip is folded in half lengthways, and then in half again, keeping the skin side inwards and the fur outside. The folded skin is pinched together hard and tied in like a feather fibre wing. Once the hair is tied-down firmly, the skin and any surplus hair is cut away. The only other material is some black ostrich herl for the head. Other furs can be used as long as they are soft and will have plenty of movement in the water.

Krieger is best known as a fly-casting instructor and demonstrator. He has taught fly casting and put on demonstrations around the world. He has been a devoted fisherman since he fished for black bass as a young man in Louisiana and Texas. When he moved to San Francisco, with his wife and two children, he became heavily involved in fly casting and won a tournament, the first prize for which was a trip to New Zealand.

It was on that first trip, some time in the late 1960s, that he saw the Rabbit. He liked the movement of the rabbit hair on the fly and shortly after returning home, he tied some long rabbit strips (4 to 6 inches) in various colours to use for fishing for black bass. These flies proved to be extremely successful.

The next step seemed easy. He began to palmer the strip all the way to the head, which created additional movement as well as being very easy to tie. Within a year, he started tying smaller ones for trout and then steelhead, Atlantic salmon, pike – everything, including tarpon. The Bunny fly is a very good representation of a leech and others have added that to the name. It also looks in the water like a small fish. Krieger believes that its effectiveness is mainly down to the fact that it has great movement, and looks alive and edible to predatory fish.

About two years after creating it, he demonstrated the tying at the San Mateo, California, fishing show and asked for help in naming it. Terrie McDonald, the wife of a fishing friend, suggested Bunny, and that became its name. Since its creation, it has been tied in many variations with Muddler-type heads to heavy bead heads and everything in between, and renamed dozens of times.

In his own tying, Krieger sometimes uses bead chain eyes, tapers the skin, and trims the bottom hairs so that they do not tangle on the hook. He also uses many different animal skins, from the original rabbit to mink, wolf, polar bear and others.

Before starting to tie this fly, select a strip of rabbit skin that is going to be strong enough and cut a long, narrow strip about an eighth of an inch wide. It must be long enough so that after you have tied it to the bend of the hook, making the tail the length that you want, you still have at least 2 or 3 inches for the body. The body is made by palmering the fur forward to the eye of the hook, where it is tied off. Krieger likes to cut the bottom of the palmered fur short so that it does not get wrapped around the bend of the hook. He says that you can finish the fly by 'tying on eyes or a Muddler head or hackle or whatever you may choose at the head of the fly'.

## DDD

**HOOK:** Wet fly, medium wire, medium to long shank, size 10–16

**THREAD:** 3/0 Kevlar yellow, tan or olive

**TAIL:** Klipspringer, deer, caribou or similar hollow-fibred antelope hair

**BODY:** Spun hair as tail, trimmed to a conical shape

**LEGS:** Pearl Krystalflash, Mirage or plain pearl Flashabou. Optional

**HACKLE:** Spun hair as tail, or brown cock hackle

# DDD

*Tom Sutcliffe – South Africa*

ALTHOUGH THE DDD IS a useful dry fly for prospecting lakes, it works very well on rivers in South Africa and, as Tom Sutcliffe has discovered, on the South Island of New Zealand and in Montana too. He first started tying it around 1976, trying to imitate a hatch of beetles he and a friend came across. Then he discovered by accident that it worked well in lakes and that if he tied it with klipspringer hair instead of deer hair, it floated better. Sutcliffe likes it in yellow, and with a collar of klipspringer instead of cock hackle, but results prove it works well enough tied with normal deer hair and a conventional hackle.

Sutcliffe does not doubt that the DDD imitates terrestrials, including moths, beetles and grasshoppers – he is not sure that it matters. The pattern bristles with enough 'triggers' to represent many different things – there is bulk in the water, yet with movement, and there is a general 'buggy' feel about the pattern as well. Like so many effective patterns, it is not easy to pin down what makes it work so well but it is improved if it is tied a little untidily or after it has been around a while.

Tom Sutcliffe lives in Cape Town and is probably the best-known fly fisherman in South Africa. He has fished extensively around the world, including Tasmania, New Zealand, the USA and British Columbia, contributed articles to many magazines and written four books on fly fishing. He is an accomplished watercolourist, of trout and yellowfish in particular, and he has illustrated some of his books. He  is also a keen ornithologist. A fellow South African fly fisherman, Andrew Levy, says: 'Above all, Tom is loved for his quiet and gentle nature and his sense of fun.'

Tom is a medical doctor by training and for many years he practised in Kwa Zulu Natal, in the heart of some excellent fly-fishing country. Tom and a young cricketer friend, Jacques, made a trip to a remote farmhouse in the Eastern Cape mountains to fish a famous stream called the Karnemelk. Tom drove downstream in his truck to save his friend a long walk home but when Jacques climbed over a barbed wire fence he ripped his leg open. The farmer brought Tom a needle and thread that he used on cattle. They gave Jacques two stiff whiskies and Tom sewed up his leg on the dining-room table. The next day Jacques was back on the river.

To tie the DDD, start by wrapping a small base of Kevlar thread at the tail end

*A rainbow trout in South Africa*

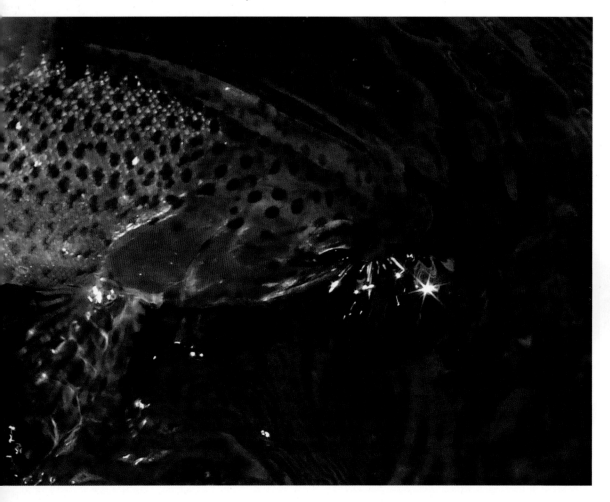

*Returning a nice rainbow trout to the stream*

of the hook and tie-in a modest bunch of hair, long enough for the fibres to extend roughly one and a half times the shank length. Spin bunches of fur along the hook shank for the body. Make sure that between each bunch of fur you use your finger nails to compress the fibres tightly. Leave yourself plenty of room at the eye for the hair collar hackle. Once you have covered the shank, tie-off, remove the fly from your vice and trim it to a roughly conical shape. Try not to do this too precisely otherwise it will look too neat; leave it a bit untidy and shaggy. Once trimmed, put the hook back in the vice. You can add the Krystalflash legs at this point. Tie-in a single strand at right angles to the hook shank and trim it so that each end is about 2 cm long. Cut about as much hair as you used for the tail and spin it at the head. Make sure you trim the butt ends of these fibres short and spin the hair with the butts pressed against the body of the fly, not the other way around. Doing it this way means that when you spin the hair the butts merge with the body and the tips radiate out, giving a really 'buggy' hackle effect.

There are a few things about fishing the DDD in streams that make this a special fly. First, the pattern is hyper-buoyant and easy to follow, even in fast, broken water. Second, the silhouette is suggestive of terrestrials and in Tom's experience, trout in freestone streams find terrestrials an appealing change from their daily diet of *Baetis* mayflies, sedges and midges. Then, finally, if the pattern is tied a little untidily, and especially if it is tied with a deer hair or klipspringer collar, it has a remarkably 'buggy' look on the water. Really untidy DDDs even have features suggesting a cripple, or at least a vulnerable insect. Trout have a way of homing in quickly on any sign of vulnerability and Sutcliffe believes that fly fishers generally do not make enough of building the cripple look into at least some of their flies and so lose out on a valuable additional 'trigger'.

He has a strong preference for yellow DDDs on rivers. This is because over the years he has got the feeling that they have a slight edge, though there is nothing like science to back that feeling. Because they float well and are easy to see on the water, he will fish DDDs in riffles or choppy runs where he would quickly lose a low-profile fly like a Parachute Adams. He also thinks that one can afford to be a little more unorthodox with DDDs when it comes to size. As a result, he uses far larger patterns than he would normally on a river. He will fish 12s and 14s, even 10s. In Reefton on the west coast of South Island, New Zealand, Zane Mirfin, one of the best guides in that neck of the woods, spent an evening watching Sutcliffe tie DDDs. His observation was that 10s were too small, that size 8s would be better and that the DDD would certainly imitate the cicada beetle. They tried it and hooked into a few pretty New Zealand brown trout.

He does dress the fly with floatant, but as with all coarse, hollow-fibre patterns, you must apply the floatant lightly otherwise it will penetrate too heavily between the fibres and even into them, and the fly will then float too low or may actually sink. As the DDD absorbs water it will, of course, slowly stop floating altogether, or just become heavier and more difficult to present gently. Press it firmly between thumb and index finger to squeeze water out, or use a pad of Adamou. Never dress a wet DDD with more floatant. But that tip goes for all deer hair patterns.

His last piece of advice is that when fishing any DDD, but especially large sizes, it's wise to leave the fly with the fish a fraction of a second longer before striking than you normally would. You will find that your yield will increase dramatically.

# F FLY

*Marjan Fratnik – Slovenia*

THE GENESIS OF MARJAN Fratnik's F fly can be traced back to the middle of the 1970s when a Swiss angler, writer and fishing-tackle shop owner, Jules Rindlisbacher, wrote about the amazing catching ability of his fly, the Entenpurzelfliege. This was the fly that Rindlisbacher would turn to when everything else had failed him. Marjan Fratnik bought some of these flies from him but it was about a year before he discovered the feathers that Rindlisbacher had used to tie them. They were, of course, what we know today as CDC feathers – *cul de canard* – which Fratnik refers to as croupions. He found the flies to be very good fish catchers but very fragile, which made them expensive as they were unusable after they had caught only one or two fish. He also found that they were not very easy to see on the water. So he set about developing a pattern that would prove to be more durable. He produced his F fly in 1983. It had no body other than tying thread or hackle and just one, two or three CDC feathers as a wing, depending on hook size.

Marjan Fratnik first publicized his F fly in the Slovenian fly-fishing magazine *Ribic* in 1983, in an article written by his friend Dr Bozidar Voljc. This was followed in 1984 by an article in the German magazine *Fliegenfischen*, this time written by Fratnik himself.

Fratnik has been fishing since 1935, when he was sixteen, mostly in Slovenia but all over the world as well, partly thanks to his job as an executive with an international company based in Milan. He now fishes F flies almost exclusively, mostly tied on size 14 hooks with natural colour croupions. In difficult light

## F FLY

HOOK: Dry fly, size 12–18, barbless round bend

THREAD: Black, or a dark colour (pink for pink version), 6/0 or 8/0 for size 18 hooks

BODY: Tying thread, or sparsely dubbed muskrat under-fur

WING: One CDC feather for hook size 18, two or three for sizes 14 and 16, and three for size 12. Trim to length of hook for slow streams and leave 2 or 3mm longer for fast rivers conditions he uses yellow or orange flies and has not noticed any reluctance of trout to take them. Yellow and white flies are also good as dusk approaches. He told me that if a fish refuses a fly after a number of presentations, he will pull his fly underwater just in front of the fish.

One version that would seem to depend on its colour is his pink grayling fly. Apparently this has a fatal attraction for grayling and is possibly the most effective grayling dry fly throughout Europe. Trout will take it as well. He got the idea for this colour from a French fly called La Lou which has a pink cock hackle and pink quill body. Like the Entenpurzelfliege, it is very fragile. Marjan maintains that one of his pink F flies will catch ten fish before becoming unusable.

Fratnik uses the word 'croupion' to describe the feathers that he uses for his fly. This has caused some bafflement and confusion. Two fly tiers, Maximilien Joset, who lived in Courtfaivre, Switzerland, and Charles Bickel in Vallorbe, also in Switzerland, produced some of the first CDC flies in 1920. Joset tied a fly called Moustique du Jura and Bikel one called Mouche de Vallorbe. These flies were classic tyings but the standard hackle was replaced with a CDC feather. Then in the 1950s the name Cul de Canard was registered by Henri Bresson who lived in the Vosges region of France. Bresson produced a fly that was a variation on the Moustique du Jura.

Marc Petitjean, who is French but lives and works in Switzerland, is largely responsible for the promotion and popularity of CDC flies today. He spoke to Henri Bresson in 1989 and decided to call his flies Croupion de Canard. This was to avoid any muddle with Bresson's Cul de Canard flies. Now Fratnik and others refer to CDC feather supplied by Marc Petitjean as croupions.

In France CDC feathers are plucked from farm-bred mallard ducks in January. They have a light khaki colour, are very transparent, strong and regular in shape which makes them easier to tie with. Once you know what CDC feathers look like and where to find them – surrounding the preen gland on a duck's back by the tail – if you have access to mallards, either dead or alive, you can pluck your own. But the quality may not always be as good as feathers from farm ducks. Commercial producers can pluck between forty and fifty feathers, which regrow every year, from each live duck.

There is still a misunderstanding about why CDC feathers and flies tied with them float so well. Darrel Martin, in his very interesting and informative book *Micropatterns, Tying and Fishing the Small Fly*, referred to CDC feathers trapping a 'sheath' of air as a result of 'embedded oils' in the feathers which made them water repellent and buoyant. Although he did mention the special structure of CDC feathers, in his opinion it was the oil that was the primary reason for their superb natural buoyancy and water-shedding qualities. This cannot be right as it would mean that the feathers could not be dyed successfully. Feathers that are to be dyed are harvested from white ducks.

The reason that CDC feathers float so well is because their structure is very different from an ordinary feather. John B. Randall wrote an interesting article, in 1995, for the magazine *American Angler*, on this subject. When viewed under a microscope, the difference can be seen easily. Every barb of a CDC feather has many long barbules on it. These barbules project from the barb in every direction and they capture and retain air bubbles when the feather is submerged. Even the shape of the CDC barbules helps the feather to retain air bubbles.

The F fly is very simple. It is tied with tying thread and between one and three croupions, depending on the size of hook, usually 12, 14, 16 or 18. Fratnik does not specify a particular make of hook, just that they should be a barbless round bend pattern. Thread colour can be black, by preference, or any other dark colour including red, olive, green or brown, and pink for the pink version for grayling. Tie a very slim body – Fratnik uses size 6 thread, except for size 18 hooks when he uses size 8 – and then take the appropriate number of feathers depending on hook size, one or two for small hooks, three or four for the largest, and their density. The feathers should be straight in the stem and symmetrical. Pinch them together with your fingers and cut the thick ends neatly and cleanly with sharp scissors. Cut them before tying them on top of the hook shank and complete with a neat whip finish. Fratnik is most insistent that to give the fly its proper form and to maintain the feathers in their proper position, you must cut the end of the feathers *before* tying them in place. The other end of the feathers can be trimmed to length, directly over the bend of the hook for slow rivers and chalk streams, and 2 or 3 millimetres longer for faster rivers. Cut them on the long side rather than too short. The head, tied as small as possible, should be finished with a drop of head varnish. Leave to dry and then varnish again.

One change that Fratnik did make to his original version was to tie it with a body of very sparsely dubbed muskrat under-fur.

*Chalk streams such as this are found only in England and in Normandy in France*

CDC flies can be real 'killers' and I have fished self-tied F flies for a number of years with great success. As with many CDC flies, some last much longer than others. I think that it depends on how much of a mauling they get in a trout's mouth. A fly that is lightly hooked in the scissors will suffer less than one inside a fish's mouth.

The F fly has all the characteristics of a truly great pattern: it is extremely attractive to both trout and grayling, it is quick and easy to tie, it is durable and it is very easy to see on the river. And above all, it catches fish.

# JABALÍ

| | |
|---|---|
| **HOOK:** | Mustad 3906B size 10–14, Daiichi 1560, Partridge SH3 or Kamasan 175 |
| **THREAD:** | Brown, 6/0 or 8/0 |
| **TAILS:** | Wild boar bristles |
| **BODY:** | Blonde wild boar dubbing |
| **RIBBING:** | Oval tinsel gold |
| **THORAX:** | Honey amber wild boar dubbing |
| **WING CASE:** | Argentine partridge or mottled turkey |
| **LEGS:** | Fibres from a small Argentine partridge |

# JABALÍ

*José (Bebe) Anchorena – Argentina*

BEBE ANCHORENA WAS ONE of the fathers of fly fishing in Argentina, along with his life-long fishing companion Jorge Donovan. He started fishing in October 1945, when the south of the country was starting to become a tourist destination and travelling was still an adventure in itself. Fly fishing – and brown trout – had been introduced to Argentina by British anglers about twenty years earlier.

His first fly rod was a heavy three-piece Hardy cane rod that he bought in a polo shop in Buenos Aires. He soon became an expert caster and, in particular, a master of the double haul. He is also an angler who can read the rivers very well and as a result is usually to be found fishing the best places.

Jorge Donovan, who devoted himself to farming, went to an exhibition in Canada in 1954. On the way back to Argentina he stopped in New York and visited a well-known fishing-tackle shop. Here he met the great Joe Brooks and persuaded him that the brown trout in Argentina were twice the size of those in the rest of the world. They struck up an immediate friendship and Joe Brooks went to Argentina to fish from 12 to 20 February that year, laden with tackle. Believing that big trout like a big fly, he came armed with huge bucktail streamers that Anchorena and Donovan called shaving brushes. He wrote of his adventures in an article in *Field and Stream*, in May 1956.

One of the first places he fished was the mouth of the Quilquihue in the Lolog. He was soon to catch a 4 kg rainbow trout. Later he said: 'In two hours I have caught the two biggest trout of my life. When I go back nobody will believe me.'

Anchorena developed the nymph in the late 1970s. The first time he looked at a wild boar skin he realized the potential for the fly tier of the crystalline under-fur. It was very similar to the once hard-to-get seal's fur dubbing. He blended characteristics from different classic nymphs like the Hare's Ear and the nymphs of John Atherton and Flick. When he was happy he called the finished pattern the Jabalí nymph.

Being a generous soul, he promptly gave Jabalí nymphs to all his friends, telling them how to dress it correctly and how to fish it, on the swing and with some tension on the line, like a greased fly for salmon. He always used floating lines and long leaders that he tied himself.

He liked the fly to be tied sparse but at the same time with the dubbing not too tight so that it has a halo of light around the body. The boar under-fur comes in different shades, from honey amber to dark brown. He always chose the honey amber colour for his nymphs. For the tail he used boar bristles because they last for ever, and Argentine partridge for the wing case and legs, although he sometimes substituted turkey feather. Normally he tied it on hooks from 10 to 14. Mustad 3906B was the hook of choice at that time, but today there are much better ones, such as the Daiichi 1560, Partridge SH3, Kamasan 175 and similar ones.

Anchorena died some years ago after a long pulmonary illness, but even when confined to his house in Buenos Aires he continued to talk about fly fishing, regaling Argentine fishermen with hundred of stories of the pioneers. He will be missed because his parting ended an era of gentlemen anglers who really set the ethical standards for today's anglers.

He took many fish over 10 lb on the Jabalí nymph, mostly on his beloved Chimehuín river. The big ones are still there for anyone who wants to give the nymph a try.

# LEONI'S BARBAROUS

*Jesús Héctor Leoni – Argentina*

FOR MANY FLY FISHERMEN used to fishing with traditional fly patterns, the thought of fishing a large nymph with long rubber legs may be the cause of some soul searching. Can they really use such a fly? What will their friends and companions say? Will they be blackballed by their fishing club? Possibly, if it is produced on the banks of the Test or Itchen, but in the wilds of Patagonia such a fly will be well recognized and its use at the right time applauded. Such a fly is Jesús Héctor Leoni's pattern, Leoni's Barbarous nymph. Prince Charles Radziwill fished the Chimehuin regularly in the 1970s and Leoni presented him with some examples of his new fly. When the prince returned to his hotel, his comment was: 'This fly is horrible, a monstrosity, but it fishes so well!'

The fly was developed in 1975. Leoni first used it for fishing the mouth of the River Correntoso in Neuquén, Argentina, with great success. He also tested it in other Patagonian rivers, including the Chimehuin (Neuquén) and Rio Grande (Tierra del Fuego), and even for fishing for salmon in Alaska.

Flies with rubber legs are becoming increasingly popular, and they do catch big fish; if they did not, anglers would not buy or tie them. On waters where they were developed any visiting angler who does not listen to local advice and refuses to use them should blame only themselves if they do not catch fish. What these legs represent to trout will never be known. Rubber legs will flex in the

## LEONI'S BARBAROUS

| | |
|---|---|
| HOOK: | Mustad 9672, size 4–8 |
| THREAD: | Black 3/0 |
| UNDERBODY: | Thread, tapering |
| BODY: | Black chenille or wool |
| HACKLE: | Grizzly cock |
| ABDOMEN: | Yellow, green or orange velvet vernille, chenille or wool |
| ANTENNAE AND TAIL: | Black rubber leg material |
| LEGS: | Three pairs, black rubber |

water and undulate to produce what we hope is a lifelike movement to the fly. Many authorities maintain that nymphs keep their legs close to their bodies when swimming and so do not include any attempt to imitate legs. Frank Sawyer's Pheasant Tail nymph is such a pattern. Héctor Leoni maintains his Barbarous does not resemble or imitate any form of trout food.

Leoni was described to me as a very friendly, well mannered, bright and joyful old man. Many years ago he was with his fishing buddy, Coco Lombardini, who was fishing successfully with a Bitch Creek, and he suggested that Héctor tried tying one with more rubber legs. During the following winter, when he was tying flies he remembered this suggestion and so he set about trying to tie an *abejorro*, a very common Patagonian black bumblebee with a yellowy-orange abdomen. He tried many different shapes and a range of materials until he finally decided on black wool for the body, an intense yellow velvet abdomen and black rubber legs, tied on a Mustad 9672 hook in sizes from 4 to 8.

At the start of the 1975 trout season, on 15 November, he cast his new pattern for the first time on the Rio Correntoso where it flows into Lake Nahuel Huapi. With his very first cast the fly was taken by a 4.4 kg rainbow trout, much to the excitement and astonishment of his friends. As a result of this very successful start, the fly soon became his favourite. He fished it on many Patagonian rivers and lakes, from Neuquén to Tierra del Fuego and also on Chilean waters from Puyehue to the rivers Serrano and Grey. He went to Alaska in July 1979 and the following year, at the suggestion of Cris Kishish, an American angler who fishes in Argentina regularly, along with Coco Lombardini and Jorge Bruzzone. On both visits his fly proved very successful for salmon. Tied on smaller hooks, it was also tested on small creeks in different areas of Argentina.

Pepe Delgado, an angler with professional interests in fishing tackle, was fishing the River Paimún with little success when he saw Leoni landing and releasing fish depressingly frequently. He asked him what fly he was using. Leoni gave him some examples of his new fly. After he had fished with them and confirmed their effectiveness, he asked Leoni if he could sell them commercially under his Boyadel brand. It was he who named it Leoni's Barbarous.

The design of the fly, with its multiple rubber legs, was quite complex at the time that it was developed. The first step in tying it is to build a tapered tying thread underbody. The next stage is to tie-in the antennae and tails and then run the tying thread back to the hook bend. The black wool or chenille for the body is then tied-in close to the hook bend, followed by the third pair of legs at two-thirds of the hook shank. Now tie the chenille or vernille under the hook shank, starting a little way back from the eye of the hook, and take the tying thread back to the legs. Tie-in the second and first pairs of legs. Take the thread back and tie-in one grizzle feather by its tip. At the same point, tie-in four strands of vernille, chenille or wool under the hook shank. Wind the chenille over the hook shank up to the first pair of legs, and tie off. Palmer the hackle over the chenille up to the front of the body and tie-off again. Finally, stretch the strands of vernille under the hook shank and tie them in at the front of the body, so that you have a complete coloured abdomen and the palmered hackle on the top and at the sides only. Complete the fly by building a neat, varnished head.

The fly in the photograph, which was tied by the inventor, has an abdomen, or belly, made from a strip of velvet, instead of vernille or chenille. The body is wool, rather than chenille. Over the years the black and yellow dressing has turned out to be the most popular combination although the green and orange variants are also very effective.

Leoni fishes the fly in several different ways, using floating or sinking lines, on rivers, for example runs, pools or river mouths, and also on lake shores where the bottom drops away sharply. Sometimes he fishes it as a streamer, sometimes as a nymph. He says that there are no fixed rules but you should use your intuition. He has fished it in Tierra del Fuego on the Río Grande casting it upstream with a floating line and letting it float back downstream as a dry fly and has caught several sea trout this way.

# MULTI NYMPH

*Lindsay Haslem, Ted Barkley and Mick Hall – Australia*

SEAL'S FUR AS A medium for tying nymphs came to Australia back in the 1930s. There were two fly tiers who played a prominent role in its acceptance, Dick Wigram and a very competent amateur called Roy Kirk. They were close friends and worked together in developing a range of nymphs to match the naturals that were found most widely in still waters and slow-moving streams. One of the patterns that finally emerged to become a standard for many decades was Dick Wigram's Brown or Pot Scrubber nymph.

When Mick Hall first entered the fly-fishing arena in 1962–3, one of the first people to help him (Hall now calls him his mentor) was the late Lindsay Haslem. At that time Haslem had developed quite a reputation as an instructor/fly tier and nymph fisherman. Later he was to move to Tasmania, where the trout fishing is still regarded as excellent. Hall kept in touch right up to Haslem's death. In the latter years they only had the opportunity to fish together a couple of times but he still cherishes those memories. Together with another keen fly angler of the day, Ted Barkley, they developed a blended brown-based seal's fur nymph to which were added small amounts of orange, green, red and yellow seal's fur. Naturally the additional colours were incorporated to give highlights and hopefully help reflect a little life into the pattern.

Hall is not sure how this pattern came into being but there was plenty of literature around from great anglers such as Skues, Taverner and Hills to provide ideas for its development. Skues blended different colours of a wide range of materials – the fur from a blue Persian cat dyed in picric acid is one of

## MULTI NYMPH

| | |
|---|---|
| **HOOK:** | Partridge Ideal nymph, size 12–14 2X long shank |
| **THREAD:** | Black 6/0 |
| **TAIL:** | Small bunch of red cock hackle fibres |
| **RIB:** | Fine gold twist or copper wire, four turns only |
| **BODY:** | Seal's fur blend: dark brown 50 per cent, olive green, black, red, orange and yellow 10 per cent each |
| **THORAX:** | Dubbing as body |
| **WING CASE:** | Mottled turkey tail fibres |

his more unusual tying materials – to create the right texture and colour of dubbing for his nymphs. The reason for this is very simple: natural nymphs are not a single colour but a blend of different shades.

But there was a big difference between the many different patterns in these old books and the patterns being tied in Australia: the size of hooks used. The Australians were tying their patterns on size 14 2X long and even as large as 12 2X long, since the size of many Australian mayfly nymphs was very well matched by hooks of these dimensions. In Australia the family known as *Leptophlebiidae* dominates many of the streams and local anglers are told that around 80 per cent of their mayfly life belongs to this family.

In the book *Australia's Best Trout Flies*, Mick Hall wrote of the Multi Nymph:

> *The father of nymph fishing, G.E.M. Skues, was a believer in blending various colours of furs, hair, or wools to create the shade or texture of dubbing required for his nymphs. So too was my mentor Lindsay Haslem and others of his association. They in turn passed on to me a number of their blend formulas, some of which have dominated my thoughts on the construction of nymphs ever since. The Multi Nymph, or 'Multi Seal's Fur Nymph' featured is a long-term favourite and has been successful for me as the years have passed. The blend in question is as follows: dark brown 50%, with the balance made of equal parts of olive green, black, red, orange and yellow.*

When fly patterns work they seem to encourage a generation of copies and the Multi Nymph has had plenty. Hall's mentor, Lindsay Haslem, was a natural teacher and one person that he took under his wing to teach him nymph fishing was the late Mauric Wilson. Hall knew him very well and even had a hand in teaching him to tie his own flies. Wilson's nature was such that when he went into something, he went in head first. He was highly organized and his camping gear reflected this: everything had a box and he even had boxes for boxes. As soon as he became proficient at fishing with the nymph, which to his credit was not very long, he gave up all other forms of fishing with a fly and spent his free time travelling from stream to stream across the trout-bearing regions of Australia fishing with the Multi Nymph. As his skills developed so did his reputation as a master in the art of nymph fishing. His reputation generated talks to numerous angling groups and at any platform he could find, he promoted the Multi Nymph.

Over time, and because of Wilson's growing reputation and that of his favourite nymph, the Multi Nymph in many areas became known as Maurie's nymph. He changed the blend slightly to suit his needs and he also promoted those features as well.

Mick Hall uses a mixture of seal's fur with a base of 50 per cent dark brown, the other 50 per cent made up of equal amounts of olive green, black, red, orange and yellow. A mix like this is best made in a reasonable quantity – enough for two or three dozen nymphs – so that you can see what you are doing. A small domestic blender will be useful for mixing everything together.

# SUPERPUPPAN

*Lennart Bergqvist – Sweden*

In 1977 Lennart Bergqvist and some friends were fishing a small river in the south-east of Norway. It was here that he first came in contact with the hatching process of a particular caddis pupa which resulted in his developing a fly that in Swedish is called Superpuppan, or the Super-pupa. It was quite revolutionary when it was first developed and today is one of Sweden's most popular flies alongside the Rackelhanen.

Bergqvist and his friends were preparing a 2 kg (4.4 lb) trout for dinner when, to their surprise, a living caddis pupa came crawling out of its mouth. They studied this strange little insect. It fought hard, with 'wave-like' movements, to break out of its pupal skin. This process lasted for at least thirty minutes, until its powers faded and it finally died of exhaustion. It was the first time any of them had seen anything like that.

The pupa was a member of the family *Rhyacophilidae* and had probably been too damaged in the trout's mouth or stomach to have the strength to hatch fully, but Bergqvist and his friends were amazed to see how much power there was in such a little creature. This species of caddis has a way of hatching which none of them had ever seen before. The pupae rise to the surface and paddle their way to the shore with powerful strokes from their long legs. On their way to the river bank, they leave a distinct trail on the surface, and since they can rise all over the width of the river, the highest concentration of food for the fish is near the shore. Therefore you can see large numbers of fish – and some really big ones – lining up close to shore to dine. When this happens, they are totally

## SUPERPUPPAN

| | |
|---|---|
| **HOOK:** | Mustad 9433, size 12 |
| **THREAD:** | Black 6/0 |
| **ABDOMEN:** | Fly-Rite No. 9 |
| **THORAX:** | 60 per cent Fly-Rite No. 2 and 40 per cent Fly-Rite No. 26 |
| **HACKLE:** | Dark dun, cut flat on the top and bottom |

selective, concentrating on the swimming pupae, and will not let themselves be fooled by something that might look like the real thing but leaves the wrong signature on the surface of the water.

Bergqvist and his friends tied a variety of pupa imitations, some traditional but tied on dry-fly hooks, and some with a hackle around the front. None of these creations worked to their satisfaction, however. They kept on for a few years, trying different ideas of how best to imitate the swimming pupa but without any worthwhile results. Then in 1983 Bergqvist abandoned his efforts to imitate the insect's appearance above the water and started concentrating on the imprint they make on the surface. He concen-

*Swedish Lapland – the land of the midnight sun and countless numbers of rivers, streams and lakes*

trated on the colours, and the way they change over the body, along with the pupa's long dark legs.

When he started fishing with his new fly he was not sure whether it should be stripped over the surface or just left to float along with the current, like a traditional dry fly. He soon realized, however, that stripping was not necessary. The imprint on the surface worked perfectly and he landed eight fish, most of them over 1 kg in weight. And this was not just a one-time fluke. The fly has proved its efficiency over and over again, on different kinds of fish in various places over the world.

The efficiency of this floating caddis pupa imitation, combined with its simplicity, earned it its name.

# 007

*Ken Orr – Australia*

THE 007 NYMPH WAS created as a still-water fly in 1988 but its universal and international success has made it the favourite nymph of its creator, Australian lodge operator and guide Ken Orr, for all occasions. He has said: 'The 007 nymph is a beauty and has proved itself to be lethal in river, stream and lake.'

Ken Orr has used it with good results on the Snake River in Wyoming but he adds a bead head or weights the nymph for the bigger rivers with heavier flows. The fly also found its way to New Zealand some years ago, via clients who had fished it in Tasmania, and is now a regular pattern in many guides' fly boxes. It is also popular in the USA, Canada and Japan.

Orr is a third-generation fly fisherman who was taught to cast a fly by his father at the age of seven. He has been a fly fisher for almost fifty years, fishing all over Tasmania, mainland Australia and overseas. He has represented Australia on nine occasions fishing in Commonwealth Fly-fishing Championships and 'one fly' events in Canada, America and New Zealand. He has been a professional fly-fishing guide and tutor for twenty-nine years, teaching, coaching and guiding anglers from all corners of the world.

He is currently a member of the Board of the Freshwater Fishing Museum and Anglers' Hall of Fame, working to preserve Australia's angling history and present it in a way that both layman and angler can understand. Ken's love for Tasmania and its trout fishery is reflected through his lifelong hobbies, sports and professional involvement in freshwater angling, although he has been

## 007

| HOOK: | Mustad 3904A, size 12–16 |
|---|---|
| THREAD: | Black monocord |
| WEIGHT: | Optional, lead wire or bead head |
| TAG: | Hot orange Glo Bug yarn |
| RIB: | Fine blue wire |
| BODY: | Black seal's fur |
| WING-CASE: | Crow wing fibres |

tempted many times in many places around the world to pursue saltwater species with the fly.

While he was developing and refining the pattern, he tested it under polaroiding conditions until he 'felt the trout sipped it in as though it was the most natural thing in the world'. He kept the pattern a secret during its early years and it was not until he fished with a Scottish client that it was given a name. The client had just caught his eighth fish in a row and turned to Ken and said: 'Crikey, lad, this is a licence to kill.' This was the spur for the 007 name.

When he was developing the fly, he was not looking at any particular representation, but it could be a water beetle, a water boatman, a floating snail or a form of stick caddis. He and his clients spent most time concentrating on the fish's reaction when approaching the fly in very clear water. Without doubt the fluoro red tag acts as a trigger for Tasmanian brown trout and will bring them to the fly for a look. At this stage, the fish would come to the fly, stop and inspect and then about 70 per cent would take it. The key to the recipe was the blue ribbing which changed the fish's reaction completely.

Fish now approach and, without stopping, pick up the fly as though it is the most natural thing in the world with a take rate of about 85 to 90 per cent. They tried many different colours and combinations over a full season but the blue rib was the real killer. The fly had to be fished inert, hanging some 4 to 5 inches below a dry fly presented to sighted browns feeding in shallow water. Its success has been almost frightening and it would not have been released in the book *Australia's Best Trout Flies* had not another ego-driven fly tier tried to rename it and lay claim to it. Ken Orr wanted to set the record straight but in so doing created what is now arguably Tasmania's most successful nymph pattern. The Scotsman who named the fly fished with Orr in February 1990, so while the fly was born some two years earlier it had been fished without a name until that February day.

In rivers Ken feels they take it for a black riffle beetle or even small stonefly 'but whatever, it still works handsomely'.

# BUSEN

**HOOK:** Streamer, size 8–18
**THREAD:** Brown, yellow or black
**ABDOMEN:** Dun seal's fur
**THORAX:** Dark brown seal's fur

# BUSEN

*Johan Klingberg – Sweden*

JOHAN KLINGBERG IS A teacher of mathematics and science in the south of Sweden. He fishes mainly for brown trout in rivers and streams and writes for the magazine *Flugfiske i Norden* and the Swedish sport-fishing organization's magazine as well.

In the early 1980s he fished a lot for stocked rainbows in natural ponds and lakes in his native Sweden, where fishing with imitative patterns was very important. This was also a time when Swedish fly tying and fly fishing were starting to develop their own methods, and moving away from the American or English ways. Swedish anglers found a way of making flies and fishing them that was suited to their own waters and fish. Over the whole of the season, although upwing flies are used, caddis or sedges are the most common fly and the primary food source for brown trout. The importance of the different natural sedges has led to the development of famous Swedish flies such as the Streaking Caddis, the Superpuppan and the Rackelhanen, all imitations of different stages of sedge flies.

One of the most important imitations for a Swedish angler is a well-tied sedge pupa. There were many different schools of thought on how to tie the best, one of which was to consider transparency, movement and the ability of the artificial to trap air bubbles. It was these ideas that led Klingberg to develop the Busen. The name means something like a tough or a tricky guy.

The first choice was the selection of material for the body. Seal's fur stood out because when dubbed on the tying thread it will trap lots of air, and if tied sparsely it produces a good impression of transparency and the fibres move gently.

There are two types of Busen: one is tied as a floating sedge pupa and the other is tied as a slow sinker. To tie the floating version, the dubbing should be tied to make a good fat abdomen which will help to keep the fly afloat. The thorax is normally tied with darker seal's fur but not too hard and tight, so that the ends of the seal's fur stick out like small legs. When fishing this version, grease it with Gink or similar to keep it afloat.

The other version, the original, is tied in a different way. Klingberg takes a small amount of dubbing and twists it very gently on the thread, wraps a few turns around the hook shank and then dubs another short length of thread and wraps a couple more turns. He builds the abdomen a few turns of dubbed thread at a time. The reason for making the abdomen in this way is that a part of the fibres are tangled round the thread and the rest of the length

*Busen Floating*

*A river in Swedish Lapland – home to trophy wild brown trout*

of the fibres hang loose along and around the body.

The thorax is tied so that the thread nearest the hook is dubbed tight for a $^{1}/_{4}$ of an inch; the rest should be dubbed very gently with free, sticking-out fibres. Now wrap the tight dubbing where the abdomen ends, and wrap it forward and end the wrappings with the loose fibres just behind the hook eye. The fly will have a very nice translucency, the ability to trap air and plenty of moving fibres over the whole body.

The Busen can imitate many different flies, if you believe in it. Fished greased as a floater it can imitate a winged caddis fly or a skating pupa, fished with just the thorax greased and the abdomen under the surface it can imitate most hatching caddis flies and when fished as a sinker it can imitate a caddis pupa.

## CDC SPARKLE DUN

| | |
|---|---|
| HOOK: | Tiemco BL900, size 16 – 22 |
| THREAD: | 6/0, colour to match thorax dubbing |
| WING: | Matched pair of CDC feathers |
| TAIL/SHUCK: | Mayfly brown Z-lon |
| ABDOMEN: | Turkey biot, dyed PMD |
| THORAX: | Rabbit or beaver fur dubbing, dyed PMD |

# CDC SPARKLE DUN

*Craig Mathews and Layne Hepworth – USA*

A TROUT LIKES AN easy meal. And a trapped mayfly is one of the easiest meals. The CDC Sparkle Dun imitates a mayfly emerging from its nymphal stage that has got stuck in its nymphal shuck. The fly is at its most effective on spring creeks and similar smooth waters, and can be used to imitate a range of mayflies such as the pale morning dun (PMD), *Beatis*, *Calibaetis*, mahogany dun, *Epeorus* and even small grey and green drakes. Fish it when trout are nymphing near the surface, taking emergers, stillborns and trapped duns. Like so many good flies, it is a very versatile and adaptable pattern and has proved its efficacy around the world.

It was designed originally by Craig Mathews, with a hair wing which makes it a more effective pattern on freestone-type waters where good flotation is more critical than the impression of a pattern on slower-moving water. Layne Hepworth was responsible for producing the CDC version with a turkey biot abdomen and CDC for the wings. As the fly has no hackle it will float on or in the surface film but will still be visible because of the wings.

In their book *Fly Patterns of Yellowstone*, Craig Mathews and John Juracek described how they had seen PMDs emerging at the crossover fence to the Harriman Ranch on Henry's Fork that included many stillborn flies coming downstream. Most of them were still attached to their nymphal shucks and

*A mountain stream in South Africa under a threatening sky*

these shucks 'sparkled and shimmered in the light'. They had used stillborn patterns of Swisher and Richard, but with only limited success. They felt that the sparkling and shimmering shucks were the trigger to the rise to the stillborn PMDs. Darrel Martin claims that 'the shimmer attracts trout and the crinkle traps bubbles'. They were convinced that the sparkle poly used for the shuck was the most effective material for the key part of their then new pattern.

The fly is easy to tie if the correct materials are used. Tie the matched pair of CDC feathers for the wings first. The length of the wing should be the same as that of the hook shank. The tail, or shuck, is tied next, using olive-brown sparkle poly yarn, or Z-lon which Mathews and Juracek popularized, and not Antron. The shuck should be between half the length of the hook shank and the full length but do not make it too bulky. Finish the fly by tying a fine, tapered body using rabbit or beaver fur dubbing, dyed the appropriate colour.

Sparkle duns can be tied with dubbing, biots and thread over Z-lon shuck bodies, particularly for hook sizes of 20 and smaller. The colour of dubbing can be selected to match the naturals being imitated.

It is most likely that this pattern was brought to England by John Goddard in the late 1980s, at about the time that Mathews and Juracek were developing it. Mathews and Goddard fished it together in Montana with great success. Goddard found the original hair-wing version to be very popular with grayling in the UK and this pattern was the inspiration for his Super Grizzly Emerger.

## CH CADDIS

| | |
|---|---|
| HOOK: | Grub hook, size 14–18 |
| THREAD: | Black, 8/0 |
| UNDERBODY/WEIGHT: | Thin brown copper wire |
| RIB: | Tag end of copper wire used for underbody |
| BODY: | Olive acetate floss |
| THORAX: | Hare's fur |
| WING CASE: | Slip from the brown side of a female paradise shellduck feather, or Décor Madeira thread, colour 1456, if you cannot find the right duck feather |

# GH CADDIS

*Gary Harlen – New Zealand*

THE GH CADDIS NYMPH was created by Gary Harlen of Hastings, New Zealand, in about 1980. He did not give it a name but Derek Quilliam, who told me about the pattern that he considers to be 'the most effective nymph ever created in the history of fly fishing', and his fishing companions have always referred to it as the GH Caddis, not to be confused with John Goddard and Cliff Henry's G & H Sedge (also known as the Goddard Caddis).

Gary Harlen's future as a fisherman was predetermined. He was the second eldest of five boys and spent his early years at Napier's Clive Estuary, where he and his brothers fished for the best part of the day or evening. By the age of ten, he had a bicycle and independence. Along with two brothers, he decided to explore the pleasures of trout fishing. Cycling 15 km with spinning rods and a great deal of determination, they became hunters of the mostly elusive brown and rainbow trout dominating their nearest river, the Tuki Tuki. He started working at the age of fifteen and when he was sixteen he had bought his first car and was able to explore and fish further afield, mostly on his own. He enjoyed the solitude of the river, away from the cramped and often violent conditions of the freezing works where he worked. By now he had become 'hooked' on the challenge of river fishing and bought his first fly rod. Getting to grips with fly fishing took him a very determined and dedicated three months, before the first fish was landed, a 'huge' $1^1/_2$ lb. But progress had been made.

Despite his enthusiasm and determination, his catches continued to be few and far between. Although he was frustrated he was not prepared to relinquish what had become a pleasurable weekend pastime, and he began to study the environmental conditions of his prey. To his amazement the flies he was using were not remotely like anything on their menu. So it was back to study. The local library was graced with his presence over the ensuing weeks as he borrowed book after book on trout fishing. A whole new world was revealed to him. Armed with information that for the first time in his life had some relevance, he was ready to go into combat. The first tactic was to tie some small wet flies like the March Brown and Hardy Favourite. Success! He caught several rainbows from 3 to 5 lb but he had not yet landed a brown.

The next development was to teach himself to tie nymphs. To begin with, these were only basic patterns, but they worked. The elusive brown was no longer elusive. A floating line was his next purchase, which enabled him to fish upstream, from behind the fish. This method changed fishing for him overnight. He could now deliver the fly to fish that he could see already. The number of catches improved substantially. As his skill increased so did his expectations of refining the art of trout fishing. He became obsessed with creating a fly which would deceive all. And so with some trial and error the GH Caddis nymph was created. Its first outing was on the Manganuku, a stream that was difficult to fish. But in the first pool he landed eight fish. He has been using this pattern for the last thirty years, and it has created considerable excitement among other dedicated fishermen. But as all fishermen know, a perfect fly is only as perfect as its presentation. Harlen is now a well-known fisherman and trout guide in Hawkes Bay. He has guided clients from many parts of the world, some of whom are now regulars.

Designing the fly was a challenge. Harlen did not want to replicate any one food source, he wanted to imitate many with one design. The food items that he wanted it to look like were mainly caddis and mayfly as these are the staple diet of trout. But he also wanted to incorporate the effect of a water boatman, a stonefly and a snail. He considered how, on the drift, each of the above would appear to the trout. He appreciated that the nymph, viewed as one food source drifting past, might not be what the trout were feeding on, but viewed from a different angle, it might appear to be something completely different.

The materials he chose had to produce a lifelike appearance. He tried a number of materials for the body but acetate floss proved to be the best, as it gave the body shape he wanted. Floss has the added benefit that it changes colour when wet. Tan is all right but he found that olive had a greater strike

*Paradise shellduck feather*

rate. The thorax is tied with hare's fur to give a rough, spiky look to emulate legs. For the wing case he tried a number of materials but found a slip of feather from a female paradise duck was the best, as it holds small bubbles of air that release as the fly drifts downstream. The correct feather is grey on one side of the stem and a ginger-brown on the other side. It is the brown side of the feather that is needed. As most river insects rise to the surface on a bubble of air, this effect gives the nymph a more lifelike image. He believes that this makes a big difference to the hit rate. The same fly with a pheasant-tail wing case does not work in the same way. Although he maintains that the paradise duck feather holds tiny bubbles of air, which Derek Quilliam reckons that the trout can see but not the angler, Quilliam suggests that a thread called Décor Madeira, colour 1456, is a good substitute if you cannot find the right duck feather.

Harlen tried hundreds of flies before he arrived at this design, which he now believes to be a super-natural releaser. It can also be used as an emerger. Just grease the leader and leave about 4 inches of tippet untreated.

This fly is best tied on a grub hook size 14, 16 or 18, quite short so that the body does not crowd the gape. On a size 14, the body should be similar in size to a body tied on a size 16. The acetate floss is tied on at the head of the fly, wound back to the bend and then forward again. The rib should be tied with wider turns as you approach the eye of the hook. The thorax is a pinch of hare's fur, rough and spiky. The wing case is tied on so that the shiny side is uppermost.

# GREENWELL'ISH PARACHUTE

| | |
|---|---|
| **HOOK:** | Dry fly, size 10–18 |
| **THREAD:** | Danville pre-waxed yellow or pale olive |
| **BODY:** | Waxed yellow or olive tying thread |
| **TAIL:** | Fibres of natural red or Greenwell cock hackle |
| **RIB:** | Fine silver wire |
| **WING POST:** | CDC feathers |
| **HACKLE:** | Natural red or Greenwell genetic cock hackle |

# GREENWELL'ISH PARACHUTE

*Stevie Munn – Northern Ireland*

GREENWELL'S GLORY MUST BE one of the world's best-known trout flies. It is uncertain how it came about, but a number of facts are known. Everyone who is interested in the history of fly fishing will agree that it was invented by Canon William Greenwell of Durham in 1854. And it would seem that the idea for the fly came to him on a fishing visit to Scotland, to fish the Tweed at Sprouston. He was having a very thin time of it, failing to catch fish that were feeding greedily when the water was alive with March browns but ignoring his artificial. He managed to catch some of the flies the fish were feeding on and decided that a good imitation would be 'wings, the inside of a blackbird's wing, with a body of red and black hackle, tied with yellow silk'. He had some flies tied by Jimmy Wright, a local fly tier, and the next day he had as fine a day's sport as he could remember.

Although in a letter to R.B. Marston, editor of *The Fishing Gazette*, Canon Greenwell included part of the dressing for his Greenwell's Glory – he did not include the hackle – he wrote that Mr Wright, fly dresser, of Sprouston, Kelso, could supply the proper dressing. Greenwell's Glory seems to have started life as a traditional wet fly, but it has been produced in endless variations as a dry fly and nymph. The only common element seems to have been the waxed yellow silk used for the body of the pattern. So Stevie Munn has followed a well-trodden path in developing his own modern version.

He lives in Co. Antrim in Northern Ireland. He was first taught to fish and tie flies, when he was about six years old, by his father, who was a very keen angler and fly tier. Although he has since fished most of Ireland's most famous loughs, his first love is river fishing for wild brown trout. To date this love has taken him to Canada, Finland, Norway, Wales, Scotland and England. He runs an angling website, is a qualified casting instructor and fishing guide and has

*The River Maine in Co. Antrim, Northern Ireland*

taught fly tying for the Belfast Institute of Further Education for over ten years.

He and his father were introduced to parachute flies when they watched a television programme by John Goddard and Brian Clark called *The Educated Trout*. Afterwards they both dressed a number of traditional patterns with parachute hackles with some success. Munn is a great fan of Greenwell-style flies and his Greenwell'ish Parachute has produced thousands of trout over the seasons, particularly when any member of the olive family is on the water. It is a consistent pattern that he cannot rate highly enough. Although any post material can be used, he uses CDC because it looks nice.

When he has tied-in the hackle fibres for the tail, and the rib, he strips the fluff from the bottom of the CDC feathers that he is going to use for the wing post. They need to be about one and a half times the hook gape in length and should be tied to the hook approximately one third of the length of the hook shank behind the eye. Pull the wing back gently and wrap the thread tightly in front of the base of the wing post. Reinforce the post with a series of thread wraps up and down the base and then add a drop of head cement to the thread base of the wing post to strengthen it.

The body is made from the tying thread and then ribbed. Tie-off the rib and tie-in the hackle behind the wing post. As the wing post will be quite soft, hold it by the tip as you wrap each successive turn of the hackle under the preceding one. Now all that remains is to tie-off the hackle, cut off the surplus and then build and cement a neat head to finish the fly.

# KILLER

| | |
|---|---|
| HOOK: | Daiichi 2220 or 1750, Mustad 79580 or 9674, size 4 |
| THREAD: | Tan or white 3/0 monocord |
| RIB: | Medium French gold oval tinsel |
| BODY: | Dirty yellow, rust or orange ultra chenille |
| WINGS: | Black or dark olive marabou |
| TOP OF WING: | Peacock herl |
| HEAD: | Deer body hair, natural and orange, tied Muddler style |

# KILLER

*Marcelo Morales – Argentina*

MARCELO MORALES HAS ALWAYS liked low-water salmon flies, so after many years he tied some streamers and Muddlers, low-water style. The Killer is a low-water Muddler fly which incorporates in the design shapes, details and colours of some other Muddlers such as the Sportsman Muddler and the Marabou Muddler which he has found to be very effective over the years. As it is a low-water tie, it never fouls during casting, which is very important in Patagonia, where the winds can be very strong. Also the position of the point of the hook in relation to the wing means that there are very few short strikes and at the same time the fly sinks faster thanks to the bigger hook. The original Muddler fly, on which Mareles based the Killer, was created by Don Gapen, in 1937 (see p. 62).

Morales fishes the fly mainly in crab-infested waters with a dead drift close to the bottom. The Patagonian crabs, also known as *pancoras* (*Aegla sp.*), are false crabs found only in South America and are the prime food source for the big browns in rivers like the Chimehuín, Caleufu and Malleo, plus many others. The *pancora* is shorter and wider than a crawfish and normally hides under rocks. They can swim quite fast with short legs flipping the stumpy tail under the body. It is easy to tell when trout are eating *pancoras* because the crabs can be felt inside a fish by touching its stomach gently. They feel just like stones. Many Argentine flies are tied to imitate them. Although they are a primary source of food for brown trout, some rainbows eat them as well, particularly those that live in lakes.

Sometimes Morales will cast the fly directly upstream and fish it just like a nymph with spectacular results. He ties it with black or dark olive wings and with dirty yellow, rust or orange ultra chenille bodies. He often fishes it with a No. 5 or No. 6 fast-action rod and a type 6 shooting head with 20 lb mono running line, with which line it is easier to keep in touch with the fly and feel when a trout takes it. The Brooks method of fishing nymphs is deadly with this fly in faster runs and riffles. The bigger the stones on the bottom of the river the better it works.

# KLINKHÅMER SPECIAL

*Hans van Klinken – Holland*

THE KLINKHÅMER SPECIAL IS now recognized as a first-class all-round, fast water fly for trout and grayling, as well as a very good searching pattern when there is no hatch in progress or nothing rising.

In 1971, when he was fifteen, Hans van Klinken tried his first fly-fishing experiments for Arctic char and Atlantic salmon, using his father's cane rod. But owing to his lack of experience, and the fact that his equipment was very old and of poor quality, he was not very successful. At the age of sixteen, when most of his friends stayed behind to impress the girls with their striking motor bikes, he decided to travel alone to fish the beautiful rivers of Norway. While camping on the banks of the River Lagen, he met two pretty Norwegian girls who taught him some tricks about fly fishing. He fished the area for eight full days, and when he finally had to leave that wonderful place, the older girl gave him her fly rod and reel, while the other one gave him a big box of flies. It was their present for the good times that they had all spent together. Hans was so happy that he forgot his father's old rod. Is it still leaning against that tree where he left it all those years ago? But for Hans, the main lesson that the girls taught him was that if you have a good fly rod, you really do not need a motor bike. And if the inventor had chosen motor bikes instead of a fly rod, this fly might never have been developed.

# KLINKHÅMER SPECIAL

| | |
|---|---|
| **HOOK:** | Partridge 15BN or 15BNX size 6–18 |
| **THREAD:** | Uni-thread 8/0, grey or tan for the body and Danville Spiderweb for the parachute hackle |
| **BODY:** | Extra fine Fly Rite poly dubbing No. 19 or 20, for large flies. Wapsi Super Fine waterproof dry fly dubbing, for small flies. Light tan colour or colour of choice |
| **WING POST:** | Wapsi Poly-yarn for normal and large flies; Niche silicone yarn for small flies |
| **THORAX:** | Peacock herl, two or three strands |
| **HACKLE:** | Good quality cock hackle, long enough to provide enough turns. Colour to combine well with the body. Blue dun, chestnut brown or light ginger. |

He started tying flies in 1976 and by the early 1980s he had started to create his own patterns, many of which had parachute hackles. He developed some unusual patterns and tying techniques. He found that the large flies that he had developed for Scandinavia worked very well elsewhere in Europe.

It was the Swedish fly the Rackelhanen that got van Klinken thinking about tying flies in a non-traditional way and helped him to innovate. The Rackelhanen is a sedge pattern that inspired him and gave him the self-confidence to develop his own patterns and techniques. He created the Klinkhåmer Special in 1984 while fishing the Glomma River in Norway. Although he did not know it at the time, a Swedish fly tier, Tomas Olsen, had created a similar pattern, but without a wing, the year before. And in the USA in 1986 Roy Richardson developed an emerger without any knowledge of the other two patterns. Van Klinken tried tying variations of the Rackelhanen which were successful, but he was not happy with them because he did not know exactly how Kenneth Boström tied his fly. He made mistakes which resulted in his tyings not floating in they way they should have. As a result, although fish rose to them with abandon, he missed too many takes. In an attempt to overcome the problem, he added a parachute hackle around the wing, an idea he had seen in a book by Eric Leiser. The result was his first parachute pattern.

When he arrived in Norway all those years before, a departing friend told him to fish for the grayling with really large flies. The friend had been using Red Tags tied on long-shank size 8 hooks, fished deep in the surface film. Van Klinken decided that he wanted something different and after a couple of days of thought, he found a large, highly curved caseless caddis larva, on the point of hatching, in the stomach of a grayling. He tied an imitation on a large Partridge Yorkshire caddis hook (k2B), taking the body as close to the barb as possible and with plenty of windings of the hackle, to ensure that the fly would float well in heavy water. He treated his new fly with floatant and dropped it into a dish of water to see how it floated. And float it did! But because of the shape of the hook, it hung much deeper in the water than his previous parachute flies. As he wrote some years ago, he did not realize just what he had created.

He fished it for the first time in some heavy rapids near his tent and the fly was taken so aggressively by the grayling that he was almost too astonished to set the hook. But he need not have worried as the fish hooked themselves. Not only was the hooking power of the big, curved hook outstanding, he found that small fish were not attracted by the fly. He then made some copies, with a thorax made from polypropylene dubbing, which he later changed for peacock herls. Two years later he started fishing for trout and using his new pattern outside Scandinavia – in England and central and southern Europe. He first fished the fly on the River Dee, in Wales, in 1986, with what he described as unbelievable success. Another time in England he fished a size 10 in a stretch of rapid water in the River Ure in Yorkshire to great effect.

The fly was originally called the LT Caddis, after the caddis which inspired its design and the use of poly dubbing in light tan colour. It was given the name Klinkhåmer Special by Hans de Groot who, during a meeting of the editorial team of a Dutch fishing magazine when van Klinken was absent, wanted to give it a Scandinavian-sounding name.

To fish a Klinkhåmer Special properly requires the use of a really good floatant. Although the Poly-yarn used for the wing post is very light, it absorbs water very quickly and easily. So once wet, it will sink the fly very quickly. Van Klinken recommends Dilly wax which is specially designed to make Poly-yarn water resistant. The hackle and wing should be treated very thoroughly with the floatant. When done properly the fly will be almost unsinkable for quite some time. Keep the floatant well clear of the body as this should penetrate through the surface film, which is one of the keys to the success of the pattern.

Van Klinken likes to fish downstream, as this presents the fly to the fish before they see the leader or its shadow, as can happen when fishing upstream. He also likes to use his own design of braided, tapered intermediate leaders as these give added weight and power, which makes casting a big fly that much easier and prevents terrible wind knots, which can happen so often with large parachute flies. By using a combination of a parachute and a snake cast he fishes his flies for as long a drift as possible, to give the fish, particularly grayling, plenty of time to see them. Grayling will often follow the fly for some time before taking it at the last minute.

At one time the idea of tying a parachute fly was anathema to many fly tiers; it was an almost insurmountable challenge. Extra hands were required – often provided by a gallows tool – and an extremely high level of skill. But when you know how, tying such a hackle is simplicity itself. And van Klinken spent the whole of one winter developing his own technique using Spiderweb thread. He wanted a method that would be easy to use and proof against the sharp teeth of trout.

*Although trees can hamper casting, they provide valuable cover for an otherwise exposed angler*

When he has finished tying the body of the fly, he turns the hook in the vice so that the wing is horizontal and the bend of the hook uppermost. He wraps a number of turns of Spiderweb around the base of the wing post to create a firm base on which the hackle will be wound. The hackle is then wound around the stem, with each successive turn underneath the previous one, closer to the hook shank. This ensures a tight, compact and durable hackle that is most unlikely to come unwound. Wrap the hackle from the top downwards around the stem enough times until the fibres clearly start changing direction. Wrap the hackle backwards closely before the fibres change position and you know you have reached the correct number of windings. To tie-off the hackle, pull it in the opposite direction to the wing post and secure it around the base of the wing between the hackle and the body, using a whip finishing tool. Trim away the unwanted hackle and then apply a drop of varnish to the tying thread, just under the parachute hackle. And that is the fly finished.

The body should be tied very slim – the slimmer the better, in fact  and taken well round the bend of the hook towards the barb, or where the barb would have been if you are tying on barbless hooks. To ensure a well-shaped body do pay particular attention to tying a very neat and tidy underbody when you tie-in the wing post. If the wing is left on the long side, it can always be cut back if it is too long.

This is one fly pattern where the correct choice of hook is essential to the correct tying and fishing of the pattern. And van Klinken designed his own special hook. Unlike the original dressing, which has remained unchanged over the years, the hooks have been developed. The Partridge 15BN Klinkhammer (sic) hook is described as having the classic shape for the pattern, with a flat spot where the wing and thorax are tied. It is the replacement for the GRS15ST, which was discontinued some years ago. The 15BN has a black nickel finish whereas the GRS15ST had a grey finish which was less easy to tie on. The latest hook is the 15BNX Klinkhammer Extreme, which has a more extreme bend. The new bend allows more of the body of the pattern to hang below the surface. It also has an offset bend.

# SIMMONS ATTRACTOR

*Alan Simmons – New Zealand*

NEW ZEALAND GUIDE ALAN Simmons developed this fly in 1986 when he had a group of anglers from Switzerland who were helicopter fishing the mountain rivers of the west coast of the South Island of New Zealand. At that time these rivers were quite unspoiled and were rarely fished, so fish were not frightened of anglers. It was 2 January, the weather was very warm and the fish were rising readily to most well-presented dry flies. Alan had been wondering about the many anglers who subscribed to the school of thought that says that if a fish refuses a fly then one should 'go smaller'. He always thought that it seemed logical that big trout would prefer a big fly and that it must be preferable to rise just once to a big fly than fifty times to minute insects.

Each morning, while everyone was eating breakfast in the old hotel kitchen, Simmons would tie the extra flies that he and his guests would need for the day. On this particular morning he tied up a couple of flies on a No. 8 long shank hook, using a lot of the materials off the Christmas tree which still stood in the corner of the room. His friend, John Boyles, who was guiding some of his party, scoffed at the fly when he saw it, saying it looked like a Christmas tree. But he sneakily picked one up from the table and stuck it into the patch on his fishing vest.

Later that day the two parties met for lunch and a large brown trout rose in the deep pool. It failed to take anything they offered it and at some point Boyles

## SIMMONS ATTRACTOR

| | |
|---|---|
| HOOK: | Long shank, size 8–10 |
| THREAD: | Black |
| TAIL: | Black squirrel or similar |
| BODY: | Dark brown wool |
| WING: | Elk hair |
| WING OVERLAY: | Crystal flash, pearl or pink |
| BODY HACKLE: | Black |
| HEAD HACKLE: | Grizzle |

put on the 'Christmas tree' for a joke. Naturally the fish rose and took the fly nicely and the whole moment was captured on video, including the expressions of surprise and humour at such a 'dumb' fish. This set Simmons off on the path to create a simple, effective Stimulator-type fly.

Although the fly was first known as the Christmas Tree, it was called the Chook by visiting Australian anglers, as they reckoned it was like casting the whole chook – feathers and all. As Simmons points out, this was in the 1980s when big flies were still relatively unusual. A well-known Australian fishing personality wrote an article about it in which he called it the Simmons Attractor and then *FlyLife* magazine also did an article on it, calling it by the same name, so it has now stuck. It underwent many changes as Simmons tried to arrive at a suitable pattern.

In 1987 John Goddard from the UK spent much of the summer with Alan Simmons and helped modify his original design. This was new territory, as large Stimulator patterns were only beginning to be developed. They tied many variations in an attempt to work out what was important to the fish. For example, the original body was yellow but Simmons was absolutely certain that dark brown worked much better. He tried every shade of crystal flash. Pink and pearl worked by far the best and he found yellow to be the worst colour. He also found that size was not a factor and that the bigger the fly the better – in line with his original thoughts. He settled on size 8 and while he does carry some size 10 flies, he is not sure they work any better. It is the size that is important to big, hungry fish.

The fly's great strength was that it floated high and was very visible in fast rivers, but much to his surprise it worked equally well on still water and these days has become the fly of choice for many anglers on lakes and reservoirs. A number of fishing writers and guides use it as their secret weapon. The Australian angler Steve Starling wrote in a three-page article on the fly, 'I had my best two days' trout fishing ever with this fly.'

During the hot summer months when large insects are on the water, this fly is hard to beat. It has also caught fish in Montana, Alaska, Tasmania, the River Test in England, Scotland and South America. It is now very popular in New Zealand and one tackle-shop owner told its inventor that he sold 100 dozen of it during one summer. He has also been told that guides in the know buy them by the carton!

In the height of summer Alan Simmons uses it almost exclusively all over New Zealand when guiding. It is always his fly of first choice at this time of the season and he would usually expect a party he is guiding to catch 95 per cent of all their fish on the Simmons Attractor.

To tie this fly, start by tying-in a bunch of squirrel tail or any other similar material as the tail and then tie-in two long black hackles, which can be the long feathers that are not suitable for hackles. Also tie-in a length of brown wool, preferably a synthetic mix so that it will help the fly to float better, for the body which wants to be about two-thirds of the length of the hook shank. Wind up the thread to this point and tie-off the brown wool. Wind the two black hackles over the brown wool and tie-off in the same place.

Take a bunch of elk hair and place it on the top of the fly as a wing and bind in. Then add a small bunch of crystal flash over the top of the elk hair. Now tie in two good grizzle hackles, wind the thread to the head of the hook and then wind the grizzle hackles tightly up to form a head. You can reverse this step if you prefer to wind the thread through the formed head hackle to secure it. Tie-off and cement the head to finish the fly.

# 3 PICOS

*Marcelo Morales – Argentina*

MARCELO MORALES, WHO RUNS Buenos Aires Anglers in Argentina, was encouraged to start his fly-fishing career back in the 1970s by two Argentine fly-fishing legends, Jorge Donovan and José 'Bebe' Anchorena, who shared their knowledge and experience with those who showed interest in the sport. Thirty or more years ago fly fishing was still in its infancy and relatively few people had experienced the riches the country had to offer to the fly-fishing world. Marcelo Morales first starting teaching fly casting and fly tying in 1979, when he was working for Jorge Donovan's fishing-tackle shop, which was the meeting place for the fly-fishermen of Argentina.

His favourite rivers are the Malleo, Quillén and Chimehuín in the San Martin and Junin de Los Andes area of Neuquen province. These rivers provide fine sport for dry-fly fishing and nymphing on light-line rods. As a fly tier he enjoys the challenge of designing and tying different flies for special purposes. He also builds bamboo rods and fishes with them frequently on his favourite rivers.

He designed the 3 Picos nymph to fish in the upper Malleo River as an imitation of the *Leptophlebiidae* family. There is a good population and number of different genera and species, so it is essential to have a good imitation of their nymphs. Of all Argentine mayflies, *Leptophlebiidae* account for around 44 per cent. In the upper Malleo, the 3 Picos nymph is most effective from early November (the start of the season in the southern hemisphere) until the middle of January. It is named after a mountain close to the upper Malleo River. This

# 3 PICOS

| | |
|---|---|
| **HOOK:** | Daiichi 1560 or Partridge SH2, size 14–18 |
| **THREAD:** | Danville 6/0 dark brown |
| **RIB:** | Fine gold wire |
| **TAIL:** | Coq de Leon fibres |
| **BODY:** | Dark olive dubbing from a hare's ear |
| **LEGS:** | Wood duck or mandarin duck |
| **THORAX COVER:** | Turkey quill or any dark quill section, shiny side up |

area is very different from the rest of the river. There is a lot of flat water and weeds, as in a chalk stream. The rainbows and browns are very selective, because of the abundance of food. Nymphs are a must, and it pays to study the behaviour of the naturals to incorporate the same movements in your presentation.

Morales ties this nymph in sizes from 14 to 18. For the body he uses a dark olive dubbing originally made by dyeing hare's ear dubbing to the shade that he wants. The tails are coq de Leon fibres which he uses because they last longer than others and have a very nice mottled effect. For the legs he uses wood duck or mandarin duck feathers which also have a very nice natural mottled effect but are softer than cock fibres and so undulate better with the current.

Coq de Leon fibres 'are stiff, glassy, and some are finely flecked' according to Darrel Martin. And they are among the very best materials for the tails of trout flies. The history of the bird can be traced back to a Spanish monastery in the early years of the seventeenth century. Local conditions in the mountainous regions of northern and eastern Spain seem to contribute to the special qualities of the roosters and their plumage. The birds are reared using traditional methods, running free in large, shaded areas and left in the open through the winter. Because only a small percentage of eggs – possibly as low as ten per cent – will produce a top quality cockerel, the birds are not killed and then skinned to harvest their feathers. Feathers are plucked by hand – a process known as strepping – during the first quarter of the moon. A bird needs to be at least two years old before it produces feathers of an acceptable quality. These feathers are usually divided into two major groups, *pardo* and *indio*, and then subdivided into a further five groups.

*Pardo* feathers are available in shades of brown, from dark to light, and have patterns that range from spotted to mottled. Various hues are also available: *pardo aconchado* has a yellowish-brown, mottled circular pattern while *pardo corzuno* has a fine, very dark brown mottled pattern. *Indio* feathers have plain or slightly spotted designs and are available in a wider range of colours and shades. They are less popular than *pardo* feathers because fewer are produced and they are less colourful.

Morales normally uses spade feathers, not saddles, as the spades have a much nicer colour and shine than the saddle hackles. He prefers to use the following colours: *pardo corzuno, pardo sarrioso* and *pardo encendido*. When choosing feathers, he looks for the very fine mottled ones as the fibres look nicer in small nymphs. He also use other colours of *pardo* in which the background is brown, like *pardo encendido*. This is a killer on adult caddis imitations.

For the legs he uses wood duck fibres, the same fibres you would use for the wings of a Quill Gordon. He likes feathers with medium stiff fibres that last much longer than soft fibres.

The 3 Picos nymph, as well as being designed to match a specific natural, is also a good general impressionistic nymph that serves Marcelo Morales very well in many different rivers and even some lakes.

# CDC & ELK

*Hans Weilenmann – Holland*

HANS WEILENMANN STARTED TYING and fishing his CDC & Elk in 1992. The inspiration for the pattern was Al Troth's Elk Hair Caddis. Originally the CDC & Elk was meant to be a dry caddis imitation, but it has since turned out to be very much more than simply a 'better' caddis pattern. It is Hans's most productive fly during mayfly (ephemerid) hatches, and his search pattern of choice when there are no hatches. He will even fish it as a wet fly. He has described it as a two-material, two-minute-to-tie pattern.

Although the fly is called CDC & Elk, it is actually tied with deer hair, not elk. According to Hans, when he donated some samples to the Catskills fly-fishing museum in Roscoe, New York State, in November 1993, he had to sign a release form, relinquishing all rights to the samples. When it came to the pattern's name, he had to think quickly while completing the form. He decided to retain the link to the inspiration of Al Troth's Elk Hair Caddis, at the same time as indicating the other key component, the CDC feather. Although the two patterns use different hair, the name has stuck. As Hans says: 'Once the name was documented as such, there was no turning back.'

Since 1992 Hans Weilenmann has found new applications for his fly and new conditions under which it has proved to be a very effective fish catcher. His experiences have been mirrored by many anglers around the world, across a wide range of rivers and water types. During the summer of 1994 he fished for six weeks in Washington, Montana and Idaho, on nineteen different rivers. On seventeen it proved to be his best pattern, easily out-fishing others he had tied.

# CDC & ELK

| | |
|---|---|
| **HOOK:** | Tiemco 102Y, or equivalent dry fly hook, size 11–17 |
| **THREAD:** | Brown 6/0 |
| **BODY/HACKLE:** | One (Type 1) CDC feather |
| **WING/HEAD:** | Fine-tipped mule deer hair, well marked with a light body and fine black tip |

As good as the Elk Hair Caddis is, Weilenmann believed that he could improve it. He claims that his fly floats better, as all the materials contribute to its floating ability and the straggling CDC barbs add movement and an illusion of life. They could represent a trailing shuck, straggling legs or antennae. He fishes it as an emerger or even a wet fly – true versatility.

In the summer of 2000, Hans fished in Montana, Idaho and Utah. He fished his CDC & Elk to the exclusion of most other flies on fourteen rivers and streams. Although the rivers were low, the weather hot and hatches very rare, he landed hundreds of trout, all but five of which were caught on the CDC & Elk. The following year west-slope cutthroats in British Columbia and brook trout in Alberta were happy to add the fly to their diets.

What Hans likes best about CDC feathers is the mobility of the barbs, whether moving in the air above the surface of the water or in the water currents in the film or subsurface. CDC feathers positioned above the surface film do not make any contribution to the buoyancy of a pattern, but they do offer a full silhouette without bulk and respond to the slightest breeze to suggest life. Submerged, CDC barbs respond to every shift in current, again suggesting life. This is where natural or dyed CDC shines, making it such an excellent choice for a broad range of patterns. With the correct choice of the material and correct treatment on the river, CDC flies can be some of the most durable patterns.

It is worth repeating how and why CDC feathers perform in the way that they do. Although ducks will transfer oil to the feathers surrounding their preen gland when grooming and preening their feathers, it is the structure of the CDC feather that gives it its buoyancy. If it was only the oil that made the feathers float, it would not be possible to dye them. As long as the structure is not damaged or degraded during the dying process, dyed feathers do retain their floatability characteristics. When a feather becomes thoroughly soaked or matted with fish slime, it will not float, which demonstrates the importance of its structure. If it was oil that made it float, this structural collapse would not matter. As long as the feather's structure is maintained, the surface area of the barbules in the film works to keep the fly afloat and the tiny air bubbles retained in the ribbon-like, kinked structure of the hydrophobic barbules hold up those barbs that have broken through the surface film. It should now be evident why we never apply any floatant to a CDC fly as so doing will cause the feather's structure to be compromised.

Hans recommends improving the floatability of the fly by using some paste floatant on the wing and head only – *never* on the CDC feather itself. When the CDC becomes wet and slimy, wash the fly well, dry it on an amadou patch or with a handkerchief and then complete the drying process with some vigorous false casts. The fly is designed to ride in the surface film with the CDC barbs providing some mobility and the illusion of life.

*A slow death for two damselflies trapped in a spider's web*

Other fly tiers have taken Hans's original concept and developed it into a wide range of variants, including diving and crippled versions, CDC & Elk spinners, emergers, wet flies and even streamers, and a mayfly (*E. Danica*), cricket and cranefly version.

Hans specifies what he describes as a Type 1 CDC feather. He developed his own system for identifying the different types and shapes of CDC feathers. A type 1 resembles a partridge body feather. It has a rounded tip and a fairly short, tapered stem with the barbs set at approximately sixty degrees to the stem. He wraps one of these around the hook shank to produce the body and trailing filaments for this pattern.

As well as Hans's original colour combination of a natural CDC feather and mule deer hair that is well marked with a light body and fine black tip, other colour combinations have proved equally effective over the years, including cream and orange deer hair and grey, yellow and orange CDC. I am sure that grayling would appreciate a pink version.

*Green Chenille Pupa*

## CHENILLE PUPA

HOOK:         Light wire, short shank Kamasan B160, size 12–14
THREAD:      Colour to match species being imitated, tan or olive
BODY:         Medium-sized Scandinavian Caddis Chenille, colour to match species being imitated
THORAX:     Sparkling antron, colour to match species being imitated
WING BUDS:  Flattened, dark brown super chenille
HACKLE:      Light brown cock hackle

# CHENILLE PUPA

*Matti Huitila – Finland*

THE CADDIS AS A species differs from *Ephemeroptera* in that they go through a complete metamorphosis – egg, larva, pupa and adult – and hatch from early spring right through to the end of autumn. Another difference is that they can feed and drink, and live for a few weeks.

Matti Huitila has always been interested in nature. When he was young he spent hours watching cased caddis larvae crawling on the bottom of the shoreline of the lake at his grandparents' summerhouse. When he started fly fishing he concentrated on trout. He has always tied his own flies because he 'had a kind of need' after his first fishing summer, to imitate events happening around the stream. It was not very long before he realized the importance of caddis to trout and grayling. He wanted to learn more and his search led him to the books of Lee Wulff and Gary LaFontaine.

His eagerness to understand more about the behaviour of the caddis and its influence on the feeding behaviour of fish led him to grow caddis larvae in an aquarium in the early 1990s. He was able to study everything that happened to them at close range and this gave him valuable insight. Looking at caddis pupae, particularly those that are important to fly fishermen, breaking the case and swimming to the surface, for example, he found that the bubble theory was wrong. (This is the theory that caddis pupae, as they started to hatch and head

*Brown Chenille Pupa*

towards the surface, had a bubble of air between the pupa and its case.) In 1991, Swisher and Richards' book *Emergers* was published. When Huitila read it, it confirmed his discoveries and gave him the confidence to carry on with his researches and observations.

Most of the pupae, especially during daylight, gained strength before darting to the surface. This was first thing to imitate. A caddis pupa swims to the surface very rapidly, and there is not much to imitate. The next step is emerging, which can be very exhausting. At this stage the insect is most vulnerable, not only to being eaten by a fish; a drop of water or a piece of foam on the surface may turn an emerger into a stillborn very easily. Fish are clever enough to wait for this easy, non-elusive prey in a convenient place. So exhausted or stillborn caddis were the next thing to imitate. Huitila admits that there are patterns that are better imitations of stillborns but his Chenille Pupa is a reasonable compromise.

A caddis pupa is quite distinctive. Huitila tested a lot of different materials in an effort to produce his pattern. Then he saw an article about flies with extended bodies made of super chenille. Although those patterns were nothing like the fly he had in his mind, he knew that this was the right material for his creation. He made a small-diameter coil spring from a piece of thin steel wire, which he used to help form the body, a spring with an outside diameter of about 2 mm, about 50 mm long.

Huitila starts tying the pattern by pushing a loop of 0.35 mono through the middle of the spring. Then he threads a 50 mm piece of medium-sized Scandinavian Caddis Chenille through the loop of mono. Pulling the loop between the index finger and thumb of one hand, making sure that the ends are together, he draws it with the mono down into the spring, leaving about 5 mm of the ends outside. Then he pulls the mono out from the loop of chenille. He passes the spring and chenille through a flame, rolling it at the same time between his

*Caddis, or sedge, which are one of the most important sources of food for trout around the world*

fingers and thumb. He prefers an alcohol lamp flame because it does not make smuts or soot. This burning process needs a little practice to get the best results. Now the body is ready. Normally he burns a waist and neck with a heated hobby knife. This way it is easy to maintain the body proportions.

He then takes a light-wire, short-shank hook such as a Kamasan B160 and wraps it with thread to the point of the hook. He ties-in the waist and secures it with a drop of Zap-A-Gap or similar. He then dubs some 50 mm of the tying thread with light green sparkling antron and makes three or four turns over the waist. (Partridge had a Scandinavian Caddis Selection and those colours were close to those he had observed and wanted.) Then he lifts up the foremost part of the chenille body and wraps the dubbing to the hook eye and back to the waist again. At that point he ties-in the wing buds which are made of flattened dark brown super chenille. At the same place he ties-in a few turns of light brown cock hackle over the wing buds. He divides the hackle points evenly so that they point to the sides and pulls the end of the body over the thorax. He ties it in over the neck point and then finishes the fly. It still needs some fine tuning, however. The hackle points pointing downwards should be removed with tweezers. Use a waterproof marker pen, of a shade darker than the chenille, to darken the top of the body. The choice of colours of the materials and marker pen depends on the species to be imitated.

During daylight hours Huitile fishes his Chenille Pupa using the outrigger method. Chuck Fothergill, in *The Masters on the Nymph*, described it thus: 'A brief but definitive description of this nymphing technique might be the "upstream, dead-drift, tight-line, high-rod, weighted-nymph technique".' This technique is also known as high sticking because the rod is usually held shoulder high, keeping as much line as possible clear of the water to reduce drag and extend drag-free drifts. When the sun sets, he removes any split shot one by one, bringing the fly closer to the surface while the light is fading. The peak of emergence is normally from 11 p.m. to 1 a.m. At that time he greases the fly so that it hangs in the surface film and dead drifts it over feeding fish. Sometimes he makes small, gentle twitches to give it an impression of life. If fish are eating *Rhyacophila* pupae, he likes to place himself above a suitable stone or log sticking out of the water. Then he lets the fly drag from the fast main current to the calmer water behind the stone or rock. If the fly is not taken then, a couple of twitches towards the rock will induce a furious strike.

# CHERNOBYL ANT

*Mark Forslund - USA*

THE STORY OF THE Chernobyl Ant can be traced back to an August day on section B of the Green River when guide Mark Forslund's client, Dick Peterson, was experiencing a seriously difficult morning's fishing from a drift boat. And the introduction to fly tiers of black foam played a crucial part in the evolution of this pattern. The lunch-time tally on that hot August day was precisely zero. The conversation over lunch must have been difficult. But a good guide will always have some means near to hand for rescuing the day for his client.

One of the most notable hatches on the Green River is the cicada. The night before his float with Dick Peterson, Mark Forslund had tied some new black monsters on size 6 hooks nearly 2 inches long. These flies did not have any rubber legs but segmented bodies with two black hackles that Mark clipped flat underneath so that they would sit in the surface film. Mark knew that big black flies with segmented bodies worked. Just before they went afloat again, Mark took his client's rod, clipping off the fly he had been using that morning and a chunk of leader to better balance the monster fly that he was about to tie on. After a couple of casts when the black monster did not turn over properly, Mark cut the leader back some more.

Dick Peterson's next cast presented the fly perfectly on a stretch known locally as Down Town, Brown Town. Almost instantly the fly was hit hard by a big brown

# CHERNOBYL ANT

| | |
|---|---|
| **HOOK:** | Standard dry fly hook, size 6 |
| **THREAD:** | Black, 6/0 |
| **BODY:** | 3 mm black foam, cut to length of $1^3/_4$ inches, by $^1/_2$ inch wide. Shape body with scissors |
| **LEGS:** | Four rubber legs, cut in 2 inch lengths |
| **INDICATOR:** | Yellow foam, 1 inch by $^1/_4$ inch |

that came from at least twenty feet away. It saw the fly and wanted it! That fish tried to kill the fly. And it was not the first one. During the afternoon, Dick caught and released twenty-three superb, quality fish and rose and missed many more. He was the first and so far the only person to have fished this pattern and at Mark's suggestion that he name it, he called it the Black Mamba.

That evening Mark called his boss Emmett Heath and told him about the fantastic afternoon's fishing. For some reason Emmett was not that impressed by Mark's latest creation. A fellow guide on the Green River, Allan Woolley of Idaho Falls, Idaho, saw it when he, Mark and some other guides were enjoying a beer at the end of the day. This story has it that the fly was named by another guide, Mark Bennion. Discussing the day's fishing and guiding, Allan Woolley is quoted as saying: 'It doesn't need a fancy name. It's just a damn ant.' Mark Bennion replied that it was a Chernobyl Ant and the name stuck. Woolley then tied a version with rubber legs, instead of the hackle. The combined effect was a pattern with a giant black silhouette and the added life of the rubber legs.

It was not long before the success of the Chernobyl Ant was picked up by other guides and it soon started to be fished regularly on the Snake River at Jackson's Hole and so moved away from the Green River area. A version of the Chernobyl Ant was used by the winner of the Jackson Hole One Fly Contest in 1995 and 1996.

The introduction of black foam was a godsend, as tying flies regularly with dyed black deer hair (which was what Mark was doing before switching to foam) was not a commercial proposition for a guide tying flies daily to be sure that he had enough in his fly boxes for the next day's guiding.

The Chernobyl Ant is highly buoyant, particularly when fished on big, powerful rivers, and very visible. It can be skated across the surface of a river to imitate a running stonefly such as tiger stoneflies, named after the dark bands on their legs. When these flies are hatching on western rivers, usually in great abundance, the Chernobyl Ant has a hatch to match. These insects travel from the river towards the shore where the males can hide in gravel. Chernobyl Ants can be fished dead drift, drifted and twitched, and used as an indicator with a nymph.

Over the past twenty or more years since its introduction in the mid-1980s, the Chernobyl Ant has evolved into many different patterns. The basic concept is so sound that there will be many more variations developed by creative anglers around the world.

*Black Mamba*

# BLACK MAMBA

| | |
|---|---|
| **HOOK:** | **Standard dry fly, size 6** |
| **THREAD:** | **6/0 black** |
| **BODY:** | **3 mm black foam cut to length of $1^1/_2$ inch, by $^1/_2$ inch wide. Shape body with scissors** |
| **LEGS:** | **Black Chinese saddle hackle** |
| **INDICATOR:** | **Yellow foam, 1 inch by $^1/_4$ inch** |

*A trout's eye view of an angler*

To tie a Chernobyl Ant, start by cutting the foam to the desired shape and tie it so that the first segment will be above the point of the hook. Then tie-in a pair of rubber legs, one pair on each side. Now move along the shank of the hook to the second segment and wrap tightly to help secure the foam (it has a tendency to spin on the hook until the wrap on the second segment is complete). Before tying-in the foam indicator, fold the foam in half and trim the two ends to a point, which helps reduce the bulk of the indicator. Tie-in the second pair of legs. Fold back $1/4$ inch of the body foam to make the head. Complete the fly with a whip finish. Finish the fly by adding cement where the head, indicator and legs sit in the second segment.

## CLARK'S CICADA

| | |
|---|---|
| **HOOK:** | TMC 200R, size 8–10 |
| **THREAD:** | Olive 6/0 |
| **BODY:** | Clipped olive deer body hair |
| **WING:** | Shaped Web Wing over pearl Krystalflash |
| **HEAD:** | Olive deer hair |
| **EYES:** | Black monofilament |
| **COLLAR:** | Olive deer hair |

# CLARK'S CICADA

*Clark Reid – New Zealand*

IN THE EARLY 1990s Clark Reid spent some time at the fly-tying factories of Umpqua Feather Merchants in Asia, doing consultancy work on New Zealand fly patterns. At the time, a well-known New Zealand angler called Gary Kemsley was also associated with the company and he mentioned to Reid that there was no commercial cicada pattern on the New Zealand market at the time. The cicada is a very significant insect in the diet of New Zealand trout, especially in the back country from December to March, when large trout throw caution to the wind in targeting these large terrestrial insects.

Reid has been guiding since 1982. He is a fourth-generation New Zealander who was born on the South Island and raised on the North Island. He is also one of New Zealand's best-known fly tiers and has been the head of product development for New Zealand and Australia for Umpqua Feather Merchants.

As part of his conservation work, he has been secretary of the New Zealand Federation of Freshwater Anglers for two terms. He was the founder and inaugural president of the Wellington Flyfishers' Club and Matamata Freshwater Anglers' Club and a councillor on both the Wellington Fish and Game Council and the Eastern Fish and Game Council.

I was pleased to be able to discuss with him some of the design process that he, as a professional fly designer and tier, went through when developing a new pattern. He is a strong believer in 'triggers' or 'supernormal releasers' in trout fly design. There were three main key elements he believed would be the 'triggers' on a cicada pattern. The first was the wedged-shape body. Deer-hair was the obvious material, and he still thinks the best, choice for this. Although foam is very popular now, a foam fly would float too high for a good cicada imitation.

The second key area was the wing shape and sparkle. Cicada wings, while

*The weather is not always good*

transparent, have a sheen that could out-do the prettiest mayfly spinner and so Krystalflash was incorporated under the wing to try and recreate that effect. The first wing material that Reid used was Shimizaki Fly Wing but he changed to Web Wing when Tiemco discontinued Shimizaki Fly Wing material. In his opinion, Web Wing is a superior material and the pattern was improved when he started using that wing material.

At the time the first Clark's Cicada appeared on the New Zealand scene neither Fly Wing nor Krystalflash were available to New Zealand tiers. Reid had encountered them while working at the Umpqua factory. He was very keen for the fly to be 'cutting edge' and this influenced his decision to use them. He told me: 'I guess that is one of those fly-tying lucky breaks that really proved a winner.'

The third ingredient he thought could be a 'trigger', albeit a secondary one, was the very pronounced compound eye of the cicada, so adding monofilament eyes was the final step to completing the pattern.

He thinks that the success of the fly is that these three ingredients, the primary 'triggers', are really all there is to the fly. Simplicity and direct imitation have made it a winner.

Clark Reid's standard method of fishing the pattern is simply on a 14 ft leader. The first 9 ft are tapered to 3X and the 5 ft of tippet to either 3X or 4X depending on what he thinks he can get away with. Before the first cast, he gives the fly an initial dressing of paste floatant and then retreats with a desiccant. Do this and it should float all day.

He fishes the fly to sighted fish and blind fishing, on streams and rivers as well as still waters. It has become New Zealand's best-selling dry fly, a fact of which he is very proud.

# GOLDEN REAPER

| | |
|---|---|
| **HOOK:** | Mustad 3666 or similar, size 6 |
| **THREAD:** | Black 6/0 |
| **BUTT:** | Orange |
| **BODY:** | Ginger or gold SLF |
| **RIB:** | Fine oval gold tinsel |
| **WING:** | Two yellow cock hackles inside two cinnamon dyed grizzle hackles |
| **CHEEKS:** | Yellow golden pheasant crest overlaid with jungle cock |
| **TOPPING:** | Golden pheasant crest |
| **HEAD:** | Black tying thread |

# GOLDEN REAPER

*Derek Quilliam – New Zealand*

DEREK QUILLIAM'S PATTERN IS interesting in that he maintains that it is at its most effective when fished either early in the morning or during the evening. Because he was busy finishing a book, he was not able to try the fly himself, but he gave some examples to a friend, Bronwyn, who gave it to another friend, who caught a $10^1/_2$ lb brown trout at eight o'clock on Tuesday, 6 January 1998 – quite late in the evening in midsummer in New Zealand. It was the first fish ever caught on his new pattern. That trout was mounted. That caught Bronwyn's attention and she subsequently caught an 11 lb brown on it. A photo of Bronwyn and the trout appeared in a local fishing publication. Both were trophy fish by New Zealand standards.

Derek Quilliam is a barrister who lives in the village of Clive, near Napier in the district of Hawkes Bay, New Zealand. He is the author of the definitive work *The Complete Guide to New Zealand's Trout Lures*. He has been a passionate angler since January 1976. Clive is situated within one hour of more than forty rivers, streams and lakes, many of them world class. Three are within five minutes of his home. He has been known to fish an evening caddis rise on his way home, still in his suit! The 2008 Commonwealth Fly Fishing Championship was held on one of those rivers and the angling club to which Quilliam belongs hosted the event.

Notwithstanding the plethora of superb trout fishing waters locally, Quilliam and his wife spend as much time as possible at the supremely beautiful Lake Waikaremoana living on board their sizeable launch.

The first germs of an idea for the Golden Reaper came when Quilliam was in Rotorua gathering material for his book. He was in a shop owned by Pat O'Keefe, an excellent angler and a superb guide. He saw some gingery grizzle hackles, which had been dyed by someone in the South Island and were not available anywhere else. They took Quilliam's fancy and he bought a quantity. At about the same time he had received a number of lures from Maureen Butler, including the Goldie Hawn. He was fascinated by her use of the golden pheasant feathers for the cheeks. Synthetic Living Fibre (SLF) was also a fairly recent arrival on the New Zealand scene and he was excited by its possibilities. He had also been talking to Hugh McDowell about the Goldie Hawn, and the latter had called it 'a symphony in gold'. Quilliam knew that that was what he was after – a symphony in gold.

When Bronwyn's friend caught a trophy brown with the Golden Reaper, Quilliam went to Rotorua and bought Pat O'Keefe's entire stock of these specially dyed feathers. Now, they are available commercially through SureStrike with the colour marketed as Cinnamon.

Quilliam admits that he may have been subconsciously influenced by the Parson's Glory, which is an iconic New Zealand lure. The Parson's Glory does not have a butt, does not use SLF, has a tail and a hackle collar, and originally he saw it as a completely different creation, but there are similarities. If any of the pedigree of Parson's Glory became incorporated into the Reaper it was bound to be a success, although he had not set out intentionally to do that – he was trying to create his 'symphony in gold'.

Since 1998 he has caught many browns and rainbows of 5 lb and over on his Golden Reaper. It seems to him to be a feature of the pattern that it attracts big fish, both rainbows and browns. For over six years, until November 2004, the smallest trout taken were a couple of rainbows of 3 lb. Since then, some smaller fish have got in on the action but large fish are the norm and expectation. When he fishes it on rivers at the right time and under the right conditions, it performs exactly as he would expect. One day he had fished up a particular run below a rapid using a couple of nymph patterns without any success. That puzzled him because there just had to be trout there, and the particular nymph patterns were, in his view, the most effective ever created. He changed to a sinking line and put on the Golden Reaper and wet-lined back down the run. He had gone only a few yards when he was fast into a very strong and lively 5 lb rainbow. The fish was taken around four o'clock on a drizzly, heavy, overcast day.

He fishes the Golden Reaper in tandem with a Woolly Bugger on lakes, often as early as five o'clock in the morning. When the Woolly Bugger starts catching, he knows that it is time to put the Golden Reaper away until the evening. He has always considered the Woolly Bugger to be indispensable, and if he had to be restricted to just one lure, that would be his choice, because the Woolly Bugger will catch fish around the clock whereas the Golden Reaper has

*Gin-clear water in a New Zealand river*

its optimum times and conditions. But during early morning and evening 'the Golden Reaper leaves the Woolly Bugger for dead'. I can see the Golden Reaper working really well in the middle of the night in the Arctic in high summer.

He has only ever tied the Golden Reaper on size 6 hooks but, as he says, there is no reason why it should not be just as effective on hooks between sizes 2 and 8. He does wish that his new creation was a bit less ornate. Jungle cock is expensive and the golden pheasant crest is probably not necessary, but because it is so phenomenally successful, he does not want to change anything. He prefers ginger SLF, which he maintains looks more 'gold' than the actual gold colour. If you cannot find ginger dyed grizzle hackles, he recommends dying grizzle feathers in iodine which will produce a gingery colour.

He starts by tying-in the rib and then dubbing the orange butt, followed by the ginger SLF for the body, which he finishes neatly at the head of the fly. The wing feathers are tied in by their butts and the fine tinsel rib is used to tie them down in the Matuku style. He then ties-in the yellow golden pheasant cheeks and the jungle cock. Finally comes the golden pheasant crest topping, then he forms a neat head and ties-off.

*Matuku* is the Maori name for the bittern. Bittern feathers were used by the Maoris to tie their flies (certainly in the 1930s and probably much earlier) that have since become known, at least in the northern hemisphere, as Matukas. Bittern feathers were used because they were a very good shape when wet and had a lifelike action during the retrieve. The bittern has been a protected species in New Zealand for many years, because the rapacious use of its feathers by the early European settlers endangered its existence, but hen pheasant flank feathers were used to replace it.

# ORIGAMI HATCHING EMERGER

*Jens Christian Pilgaard – Denmark*

USING A FEATHER'S OWN structure to make a wing adds another dimension to a finished fly by bringing natural curves and lines to flies, which Jens Christian Pilgaard had never seen before. He was amazed by the similarity of the wings of real insects and the artificial ones made out of a single feather. Shortly after developing his Origami wing technique, he discovered that this way of using the feathers gave him some unexpected advantages that he could use not only for very realistic flies but also for actual fishing flies. He now maintains that it is one of the fastest ways of tying winged dry flies that are beautiful as well as functional.

In 1994 Steve Fernandez from the USA showed Pilgaard how to make Otzinger and Wonder wings by folding feathers and using the stem as backbone for the wing, and by cutting the top away, leaving the front made of the fragile fibres. Right away Jens thought that these wings were too fragile, so after playing around with some feathers for a while he invented what became the Origami wing, which he named after the Japanese art of paper folding.

His sole proviso is that the flies for fishing should only be tied in smaller

# ORIGAMI HATCHING EMERGER

**HOOK:**       Any light grub hook, size 14

**THREAD:**   Thin white unspun thread that can be dyed with a marker pen to match the colour of the insect

**BODY:**       Dark brown condor, or substitute

**WING:**       Genetic cock hackle, stripped and folded origami style. Colour to match the insect to be imitated

**THORAX:**   CDC fibres dubbed on tying thread and wrapped around wing root

**LEGS:**       Surplus fibres from wing hackle

sizes because the wing has a tendency to become too stiff when it comes to winging bigger flies such as big mayflies (*Danica* etc.). Using this type of wing will give the ultimate imitation of the insect and he is convinced that it really does matter when it comes to luring the old brownie or the grayling.

Jens Pilgaard and his wife, Helle, have been running their fly-tying shop since March 1993. They started selling feathers and other fly-tying materials, as it seemed almost impossible to get hold of decent materials when he started tying flies many years ago. Now they can offer their customers the highest quality materials, especially exotic bird skins and feathers.

The only materials you need to make the simplest super-realistic dry fly are a hook and an undyed hackle with long fibres and a thin stem. Start by putting a suitable hook in your vice and then tie-in a tail and a body for the fly you want to imitate. Make sure that you leave the front quarter of the shank for the wing and hackle. Pilgaard uses only one wing per fly as this will prevent it from twisting and spinning when casting.

To make the wing, hold the hackle by the tip in front of you with the front side towards you. Strip off all the fluff at the bottom on both sides and the fibres on the left side only of the stem. At the middle of the stem give the hackle a small bend to the right and then grip the feather at that point with a pair of tweezers with flat jaws, holding them in your left hand. With your right hand, pull down all the fibres and the top of the hackle stem alongside the bottom part of the stem until the desired height of the wing is obtained.

Holding the wing in your right hand pull out the left side to a delta shape with the tweezers in your left hand, still pressing on the root to prevent the wing deforming. Then measure out the wing over the body as you would do with a traditional wet-fly feather wing. Now take the wing between your left thumb and forefinger. Be careful not to let go of the wing in your right hand before you have got hold of it with your left hand. If you do, it will lose its shape and you then will have to bend the wing into the desired shape again.

All that is left now is to tie it down as you would do with a feather wing for a wet fly; cut away the waste ends of the wing and put on a hackle suitable for the fly.

This technique is also good for small midges but do make sure to choose feathers with thin stems or use only the very top of the hackle where the stem is thin so that the wings stay as soft as possible. It is possible to make the wing out of a CDC feather, which makes it ideal for tiny flies.

The simple super-realistic fishing fly mentioned earlier is made the same way, leaving out the tail and body. Here you wrap the thread the length of the shank and tie down the wing as described above. Cut away the two ends of the hackle stem, making sure not to cut away the surplus fibres pointing towards the head of the fly. Take some of these fibres, fold them backwards alongside the hook shank and tie them in with a single turn or two of tying thread. Repeat this procedure on the other side of the hook. The rest of the fibres, pointing forwards, are divided with a few turns in a figure of eight.

*Swans look pretty on the water but they eat an awful lot of river weed, often to the detriment of chalk streams*

Finish the fly with a few half hitches around the wing root and seal it with a drop of lacquer.

Now you have a very simple but most effective mayfly imitation combining all the ingredients necessary for success: a body imitated by the hook shank; a wing of a shape that is familiar to fish; and legs. The surplus fibres are almost like a parachute hackle if tied-in correctly. Pilgaard prefers to fish this fly with the wing twisted in a 90 degree angle to the side. This improves the hooking abilities and imitates a crippled or stillborn insect.

His choice of a condor fibre for the bodies of his flies produces a nicely segmented effect. If you cannot obtain a condor feather, he suggests that feathers from any big bird of prey are excellent substitutes. He is reluctant to specify any particular brand or pattern of hook or make of tying thread, as the flies can be tied on any suitable hook with any suitable thread. Specifying particular hooks or thread simply sends fly tiers on an often fruitless search and leads to frustration if they cannot be sourced. He also thinks that fly tiers should be allowed to make some decisions for themselves.

When fishing a fly with an origami wing, do not become frustrated if your fly lands on its side. This will only signal to the fish that it is an easy prey. Flies lying on their sides are bound to stay on the surface unlike those sitting upright which are capable of flying away at any time.

# ORIGAMI TRADITIONAL

| | |
|---|---|
| **HOOK:** | Traditional dry fly, size according to size of the particular insect you want to imitate |
| **THREAD:** | Thin white unspun thread that can be dyed with a marker pen to match the colour of the insect |
| **TAIL:** | A few fibres from the same hackle as the wing |
| **BODY:** | Dark condor, or substitute |
| **WING:** | Genetic cock hackle, stripped and folded origami style. Colour to match the insect to be imitated |
| **HACKLE:** | Preferably the same colour as the wing, tied in traditional style, or on a dubbing ball underneath the thorax |

# PRINCETAIL

| | |
|---|---|
| HOOK: | Mustad 80250, size 8–18 |
| THREAD: | Pre-waxed brown, 6/0 |
| BEAD: | Brass, or tungsten – particularly for smaller sizes |
| TAIL: | Ring-neck pheasant tail fibres |
| RIB: | Fine copper wire |
| BODY: | Ring-neck pheasant tail |
| THORAX: | Peacock herl |
| HACKLE: | Brown |
| WINGS: | White goose biots |

# PRINCETAIL

*Abel Tripoli – Argentina*

AS THE NAME SUGGESTS, there are two flies in one in this pattern. What fly fisher can resist the Prince and Pheasant Tail nymphs? They can catch fish when nothing else seems to make them bite. Abel Tripoli works as a guide and fly tier for the Fly Master's Fly Shop in Bariloche, Argentina, and when he is not fishing or tying flies, he likes to play the guitar and dance the tango. He developed this pattern one day when snow was falling outside and he was counting the days to when he could get back to fishing again. He never planned to tie a fly based on these two popular patterns. What happened was that he was tying a very boring pattern when he started to look at some of the flies that he had tied already. One of them was a size 8 Prince, a very effective nymph for Argentine rivers at the start of the season. He picked it up, and suddenly in his mind broke it in two. He thought, why not combine the features of peacock, pheasant and goose to make an attractive hybrid?

What he wanted was something based on a Prince nymph but with a slimmer profile, something that looked like the shape of a mayfly nymph. He remembered that he had had to guide some Americans on the gin-clear waters of the Rivadavia River a few years ago, early in January. The first place they stopped to fish from the bank was where a little creek called Colehual feeds the Rivadavia – a very pleasant run about one hundred yards long and quite shallow at that moment. As soon as they approached they could see the head of a large shoal of rainbows spread all along the run. It was difficult to count how many or to believe that so many fish could all be in one run – and they were all feeding.

Something very important Tripoli has learned in his guiding career is to watch before acting. The fish were taking nymphs with the classic movement: sliding sideways a little, taking something and returning to their original position, over and over.

He did not have a suitable net to catch some of those little creatures that the fish were feeding on. The only thing that he could think of using was his T-shirt. So he took it off and held it in the water for a minute or so. When he lifted it up he found a good number of little mayfly nymphs attached to it. They were slightly brownish in colour and he estimated the size to be about that of a size 16 nymph hook. He had some imitations that looked similar but they were too big, and it seemed these fish were fussy about size, because as soon as his clients put on one of those imitations they headed for it but turned around as soon as they realized it was not what they were looking for. Sadly, he had nothing better to offer them from his fly boxes. They caught some nice fish that morning, but they certainly missed a lot.

That day came back to him suddenly as he watched the falling snow. The nymphs, the colour, the size – they were all similar to the fly he was thinking about. And the pattern has since proved to be a serious trout catcher, not just in the Rivadavia but in many other rivers where he has fished with it. Since then it has become one of his favourites for the Rivadavia.

When tying this pattern Tripoli suggests using a tungsten bead instead of the regular ones. He also prefers to rib the body with fine copper wire. He has used golden tinsel, which looks very attractive, but he has found that these two elements – the tungsten bead and the copper wire – help the fly to sink more quickly in fast waters, particularly in small sizes. Ring-neck pheasant tail fibres and peacock herl vary in colour and so the Princetail can be tied in different shades and colours.

# SPARKLY HARE & COPPER

*John Scott – New Zealand*

IS THE HARE & COPPER, one of New Zealand's most popular nymph patterns, just another version of a Gold-ribbed Hare's Ear? It is certainly to New Zealand what the GRHE is to Britain. Some New Zealand experts suggest that it 'sort of is and sort of isn't'. When tied large and rough, or even small and without weight, it is a very good sedge imitation when trout are taking hatching caddis. It is generally accepted that the pattern should be tied scruffy. But like the GRHE, it comes in different versions, including the Sparkly Hare & Copper.

John Scott originally created the Sparkly Hare & Copper for the Mohaka River in Hawkes Bay. It is a big river by almost any standards and it needs to be fished deep, hence the tungsten bead. In fact, like all good flies it fishes well anywhere. It is very good on the point with a GH Caddis on the dropper. Although a gold tungsten bead is the most popular, other colours are effective as well. The sparkle represents air bubbles. Scott originally tied it with a tail of pheasant tail fibres. Others, including Derek Quilliam, followed suit but found them to be too brittle so Quilliam started using ordinary brown hackle fibres. Some time later he discovered that Scott had come to the same conclusion, so that is how the pattern is tied today.

Scott is a professional fly tier and guide. He is also very active in promoting

# SPARKLY HARE & COPPER

| | |
|---|---|
| **HOOK:** | Black Magic H10, 3X short shank, size 10–16 |
| **THREAD:** | Black 8/0 |
| **HEAD:** | Gold tungsten bead |
| **WEIGHT:** | Brown copper wire |
| **TAIL:** | Brown hackle fibres |
| **RIB:** | Tag end of copper wire underbody |
| **UNDERBODY:** | Silver ice chenille |
| **BODY:** | Hare's fur |

the welfare of local rivers and streams, such as fencing to keep cattle out of the waterways, and planting trees.

Use the copper wire to produce a nice carrot-shaped body. Scott ties-in the chenille at the tail and then forms a dubbing loop. He winds the chenille forward and ties it off behind the gold bead and then puts the hare's fur in the dubbing loop and dubs the body, followed by the copper rib.

# ZAK

| | |
|---|---|
| **HOOK:** | 1 or 2X long shank, size 10–18 |
| **THREAD:** | 6/0, red, green or blue |
| **BEAD:** | Brass, tungsten or dark green glass. Optional |
| **WEIGHT:** | Lead wire. Optional |
| **TAIL:** | Five or six water mongoose guard hairs, stiff dun cockle hackle fibres or squirrel tail hairs |
| **BODY:** | Composite of two peacock and two stripped peacock hurls |
| **RIB:** | DMC or Accent Yarn thread in metallic blue or green, and copper or brass wire |
| **HACKLE:** | Dark dun or natural black genetic hackle |

# ZAK

*Tom Sutcliffe – South Africa*

No ANGLER WILL DISAGREE with Tom Sutcliffe when he says:

> You want at least one mayfly nymph that is an all-purpose pattern, the sort
> of fly you can tie on and feel confident comes close to matching pretty well any
> nymph. The pattern should, of course, be durable and easy to tie, because,
> like me, you probably put your fair share of flies into trees. The Zak nymph
> has worked well for me as a general all-purpose nymph and may well now be
> the most-used nymph on South African rivers. It has also proved to be deadly
> on large browns in the South Island of New Zealand.

The Zak nymph can be tied in a range of sizes to match the nymphs in the
stream you are fishing. Tie the pattern with different amounts of weight to suit
the strength of current and depth of water. Turn over a few stones on the bed
and you can quickly get an idea of the general size of the nymph population in
the water at the time.

Over the years, Tom Sutcliffe has changed the Zak a little, as he discovered
better materials, or better tying methods, or deficiencies in the original pattern.
The idea was to give the fly the semi-crustaceous-looking abdominal segments
of the natural with the breathing gills and, of course, the prominent thorax, with
just a subtle suggestion of legs. Overall, the fly must have movement and it must
have the right colour and shape. This means a long, wispy tail, a cigar-shaped
body, a prominent thorax with a hint of hackle, and a generally dark colour. If

*Classic pocket water best fished with a weighted nymph or a very buoyant dry fly*

those characteristics are not immediately evident in any Zak you have tied give it away, or do not buy it if you did not tie it. Particularly, discard any that are over-hackled or that have dense, stubby tails. This is not another Woolly Worm pattern, or a domestic bottlebrush.

The Zak fishes well on a floating line with a strike indicator, just like most other nymph patterns, getting takes on the drop, especially in slow-moving rivers, or drifting deep in fast runs, or tumbling in riffle water, and often on the swing-out, when you can add a little movement to the fly, or retrieve it. On small rivers Sutcliffe uses 14s and 16s, and on large ones with deep pools he may go up to a size 10. He weights the flies variously and uses a colour code to identify them: green thread for unweighted, blue for weighted and red for dangerously heavy. This way he can get the fly to drift near the top or sink like a brick, depending on conditions. The distance he positions the indicator from the fly is roughly twice the depth of the water he is fishing, and for really heavily weighted Zaks he often uses two or three indicators, at various distances from the fly.

If you like bead-head flies, add a bead to a long shank hook. Sutcliffe says 'The jury is still out on what works best.' He uses dark green glass beads for unweighted patterns and brass or tungsten ones for weighted. When tying the fly, wrap the hook shank with tying thread in the usual way but bring the thread further round the bend of the hook than you would normally. This will serve as a visible indicator of how the fly is weighted. (Many fly tiers rely on the silk at the head of the fly to indicate weight.) Tie in a sparse tail of water mongoose guard hairs, or, if you have no water mongoose, a few wisps of dark dun or black cock hackle or squirrel tail fibres. The tail should be about one and a half to two times as long as the hook shank. Add lead at the thorax, but with unweighted patterns build up a thorax with a single strand of natural wool until you get the right shape into the fly.

The body formula is, first, four peacock hurls, two of them stripped clean. Do this by stroking the hurl against the grain, held between your thumb and the nail of your index finger; you should strip only the bottom half. With a little practice it goes quickly. Second, you need a piece of shiny purple/blue thread. Krystalflash works well but Sutcliffe now uses a metallic thread called DMC Fil metalisé, colour number 4012, or blue Accent Yarn, both of which are available from haberdashery stores. Finally, add a piece of copper or brass wire, to lend strength. He ties all these ingredients in together just behind the thorax. Gather them into one bunch and wind the silk back towards the tail, trapping the bunch on the side of the hook shank as you go. This avoids an unsightly blob at the tail end, adds strength and gives some lateral shape to the body.

A vital new development is tying-in the two stripped peacock hurls by the tip of their butt ends where they are pale, almost ivory-coloured. This gives the pale, crustaceous-looking segmentation where you want it, in the abdomen, not up at the thorax.

Now gently twist the peacock hurl, wire and DMC thread but do not make too tight a 'rope'. Wrap the rope towards the thorax, fairly tightly. Stop

*An adult September dun, seen commonly on Cape fly streams at that time of year*

at the thorax and tie in a long dark dun or black cock hackle by the tip. A genetic hackle is good, because they are long and thin, but dark Indian or Chinese necks work well enough. Sutcliffe does not like dyed black hackles for this pattern. The size of hackle should be the same as you would choose if you were dressing a dry fly on an equivalent-sized hook. To avoid an over-dressed look, strip off the fibres from one side of the hackle before you tie it in. Now twist the hackle and the body rope together and wrap to just behind the bead and tie off.

# HAYESTUCK

*Peter Hayes – England*

PETER HAYES LIVES IN Wiltshire and is fortunate to be able to fish many of England's very best chalk streams – the Wylye (which he has fished since 1982), the Test, the Anton (a tributary of the Test), the Itchen and the Avon – one of nature's very best laboratories for developing and testing new fly patterns. Since the start of the last decade of the twentieth century, he has developed a number of interesting new dry flies, including one, the PHD (Peter Hayes's Dun) which, unwittingly, revived the tying technique, although in a slightly different way, that William-Powlett used for his Cocky Spinner. However, the Hayestuck is a mayfly emerger designed to represent emergent crippled mayflies, stuck in their shuck. These big flies provide one of the easiest meals for trout – often very big trout.

For a trout to grow big and fat, it needs to feed as efficiently as possible, taking in more food and energy than it expends while feeding. A trout wants maximum return for minimum expenditure of energy. They have a minimum daily requirement, known as the maintenance requirement, which will prevent them from losing weight but will not be sufficient for any gain in weight. Food consumed over and above the maintenance requirement will help them to grow. A trout's instincts seem to direct it to feed on food items that require the least expenditure of energy and the highest certainty of capture. Thus a mayfly that is attempting to hatch or, even better, that has got stuck and is emerging as a cripple, will be the most desirable mouthful for a hungry fish – a large fly that is most unlikely to be able to escape being eaten. In Peter Hayes's opinion, a

# HAYESTUCK

| | |
|---|---|
| **HOOK:** | Long-shank, light wire, round bend Mayfly hook, size 12 |
| **THREAD:** | Light brown 6/0 |
| **TAIL/TRAILING SHUCK:** | 4–6 strands of thick brown tying thread |
| **SHUCK LEGS:** | Small brown, short-fibred neck hackle, trimmed on top of hook shank |
| **RIB:** | Brown floss |
| **ABDOMEN:** | Snowshoe hare's foot fur |
| **HACKLE:** | Greenwell saddle hackle, with 'v' cut out of the bottom of the hackles |
| **WINGS:** | Two long CDC feathers |
| **THORAX:** | Generous quantity of snowshoe hare's foot fur |

trout is most likely to suspend disbelief and accept the angler's imitation of a hatching fly stuck in its shuck. Following on from this assumption, he believes that most artificial flies look more like (crippled) emergers, as their abdomens are in the surface film rather than above, as is the case with natural duns, and when an imitation of the hatched fly stops catching fish, it should be replaced with a better imitation of a crippled emerger and not a better dun. This is most true towards the end of a mayfly hatch, particularly after the peak of the season's hatch.

Like most of Hayes's patterns, he has borrowed ideas from other patterns and fellow anglers for the Hayestuck. He makes no attempt to disguise this fact and is most happy to acknowledge his sources of inspiration. The name was inspired by the Haystack, an effective fly at mayfly time, and the body from the Usual, a Fran Betters pattern that uses snowshoe hare's foot fur for maximum buoyancy. In developing it Hayes was hoping to produce an artificial fly that a trout would be prepared to swim over to inspect, if a presentation was less than accurate, and even after examining it closely, ignore the inaccuracies compared to the naturals and swallow it enthusiastically. He fished the fly on his home waters of the Wylye and Itchen with great success some years before trying it on the Piscatorial Society's waters on the Hampshire Avon. His best fish that day was a 6 lb brown trout. A few days later saw him use it on the Anton, and catch and release a 27 inch fish with a girth of 17 inches which he estimated was a double-figure fish.

When tying the fly, Hayes likes to start by closing any gap where the eye of the hook meets the shank with tying thread, before taking the thread just round the bend of the hook. He uses a fine wire brush to tease out the strands of the brown tying thread which form the trailing shuck. When he has frayed them thoroughly, he puts a spot of superglue on the ends to help the shuck to sink and prevent them splaying out and stopping the tail or shuck from sinking. The hackle wound at the tail, to represent the legs of the cripple, is clipped off on the top of the hook, leaving only the fibres to the side and below the hook shank. The front hackle is also clipped but into a slight 'v', leaving plenty of fibres pointing outwards to support the front of the fly. A generous amount of snowshoe hare's foot fur is used for the body, which is ribbed with brown floss, and an even more generous amount is used to form the thorax. Snowshoe hare's foot fur is naturally very buoyant and the colour is a good

*A mayfly trapped in the surface film is an easy meal for a trout*

match for that of the natural mayfly, as well as being reflective and translucent. The wings are made from two CDC feathers, tied in a loop to represent the half-emerged wings of the natural. Hayes often treats his flies with an 'overnight' floatant (but do not put any on the shuck) and will, if necessary, top up on the river with Dave's Bug Float.

# BIBLIOGRAPHY

Bates, Joseph D., *Streamer Fly Tying and Fishing* (Stackpole Books, USA, 1995)

Beck, Barry, 'Angler of the Year: Russell Blessing' (*Fly Rod & Reel*, USA, January/February 2006)

Blades, William F., *Fishing Flies and Fly Tying, American Insects, Including Nymphs and Crustaceans* (Stackpole Books, USA, 1979)

Brooks, Charles E., *Nymph Fishing for Larger Trout* (Lyons & Burford, USA, 1976)

Broughton, Ronald, *The Complete Book of the Grayling* (Robert Hale, 2000)

Deane, Peter, *Peter Deane's Fly-tying* (Batsford, 1993)

Draper, Keith, *Trout Flies in New Zealand* (AH & AW Reed, New Zealand, 1982)

Dunham, Judith, *The Art of The Trout Fly* (Chronicle Books, USA, 1988)

Edmonds, Harfield N., and Lee, Norman N., *Brook and River Trouting* (published privately, 1916)

Engle, Ed, *Tying Small Flies* (Stackpole Books, USA, 2004)

Farson, Negley, *Going Fishing* (Country Life, 1942)

Fothergill, Chuck, 'Advanced Nymphing Techniques', in *The Masters on the Nymph* (Robert Hale, 1994)

Gierach, John, *Good Flies, Favorite Trout Patterns and How They Got That Way* (The Lyons Press, USA, 2000)

Grant, George F., *Montana Trout Flies* (published privately, USA, 1972)

Halford, F.M., *Floating Flies and How to Dress Them* (Barry Shurlock & Co, 1974)

Hayes, Peter, 'Haymaker of a Mayfly' (*Fly-Fishing and Fly-Tying*, June, 2006)

Hayter, Tony, *F.M. Halford and the Dry-Fly Revolution* (Robert Hale, 2002)

Herd, Dr Andrew N., *A FlyFishing History: Greenwell's Glory* (www.flyfishinghistory.com/greenwells_glory.htm)

Hidy, V.S., 'Soft-hackle Nymphs – the Flymphs', in *The Masters on the Nymph* (Robert Hale, 1994)

Hills, John Waller, *River Keeper, The Life of William James Lunn* (Geoffrey Bles, 1934)

*A Summer On The Test*, (André Deutsch, 1983)

Hughes, Dave, *Essential Trout Flies* (Stackpole Books, USA, 2000)

Kaufmann, Randall, *American Nymph Fly Tying Manual* (Frank Amato Publications, USA, 1986)

Leighton, Michael, *Trout Flies of Shropshire and the Welsh-Borderlands* (published privately, 1987)

Leisenring, James E., and Hidy, Vernon S., *The Art of Tying the Wet Fly & Fishing the Flymph* (Crown Publishers, USA, 1973)

Links, Leon, *Tying Flies with CDC, The Fisherman's Miracle Feather* (Merlin Unwin Books, 2002)

Lunn, Mick, with Clive Graham Ranger, *A Particular Lunn* (Unwin Hyman, 1990)

Marinaro, Vincent, *A Modern DRY-FLY Code* (The Flyfisher's Classic Library, 1996)

Martin, Darrel, *Fly-Tying Methods* (David & Charles, 1987)

*Micropatterns, Tying and Fishing The Small Fly* (Swan Hill Press, 1994)

Mathews, Craig, and Juracek, John, *Fly Patterns of Yellowstone* (Blue Ribbon Flies, USA, 1987)

Merritt, J.I., *Trout Dreams, A Gallery of Fly-Fishing Profiles* (The Derrydale Press, USA, 2000)

Morris, Skip, *The Art of Tying the Nymph* (Frank Amato Publications, USA, 1993)

Mottram, Dr J.C., *Thoughts on Angling* (Herbert Jenkins, *c.* 1945)

Niemeyer, Ted, 'Lew Oatman: Master Tier', *Fly Fisherman*, USA, April 1981

Overfield, Donald T., *Fifty Favourite Nymphs* (Ernest Benn, 1978)

Parsons, John, and Hammond, Bryn, *One Hundred Years of Trout Fishing in New Zealand* (The Halcyon Press, New Zealand, 1999)

Roberts, John (ed.), *The World's Best Trout Flies* (Tiger Books International, 1995)

Robson, Kenneth (ed.), *The Essential G.E.M. Skues* (A & C Black, 1998)

Rolt, H.A., *Grayling Fishing in South Country Streams* (Marston & Company, 1905)

Ross, John, *Trout Unlimited's Guide to America's 100 Best Trout Streams* (The Globe Pequot Press, USA, 1999)

Sanchez, Scott, 'Invasion of the Chernobyl Ant', *Flyfishing & Tying Journal*, Spring 2001

Sawyer, Frank, *Keeper of the Stream* (Unwin Hyman, 1987)

Scholes, David, *Fly-fisher in Tasmania* (Melbourne University Press, Australia, 1961)
   *The Way of an Angler* (The Jacaranda Press, Australia, 1963)

Skues, G.E.M., *The Way of a Trout with a Fly* (A & C Black, 1949)
   *Nymph Fishing for Chalk Stream Trout* (A & C Black, 1974)

Sloane, Robert (ed.) *Australia's Best Trout Flies* (FlyLife Publishing, Australia, 2001)

Smedley, Harold Hinsdill, *Fly Patterns and Their Origins* (Westshore Publications, USA, 1950)

Steeves, III, Harrison R., *Tying Flies with Foam, Fur, and Feathers* (Stackpole Books, USA, 2003)

Stokes, Max, *Tasmanian Trout Fly Patterns* (The Tasmanian Fly Tyers' Club, Australia, 1999)

Voss Bark, Conrad, *Conrad Voss Bark on Flyfishing* (Unwin Hyman, 1989)
   *The Dry Fly, Progress since Halford* (Merlin Unwin Books, 1996)

Walbran, Francis M., *Grayling and How to Catch Them and Recollections of a Sportsman* (The Flyfisher's Classic Library, 2004)

Weilenmann, Hans, 'CDC & Elk', *Fly Dresser*, Winter 2001

Wigram, R.H., *Nymph Fishing in the Southern Hemisphere* (Angling and Gun Sport, Australia, 1939)
   *The Fly* (Stevens Publishing, Australia, 2003)

Wilson, Dermot, *Dry-Fly Beginnings* (Douglas Saunders with Macgibbon and Kee, 1957)

Wulff, Lee, *Lee Wulff on Flies* (Stackpole Books, USA, 1980)
   *Trout on a Fly* (Nick Lyons Books, USA, 1986)